VOICE OF THE BUDDHA
THE DHAMMAPADA

BUDDHISM FOR THE COMMON READER

VOICE OF THE BUDDHA
THE DHAMMAPADA

BUDDHISM FOR THE COMMON READER

With a foreword by His Holiness the Dalai Lama

Shiv K. Kumar

ATLANTIC

PUBLISHERS & DISTRIBUTORS (P) LTD

Published by
ATLANTIC
PUBLISHERS & DISTRIBUTORS (P) LTD
7/22, Ansari Road, Darya Ganj, New Delhi-110002
Phones : +91-11-40775252, 40775214, 23273880, 23275880
Fax: +91-11-23285873
Web: www.atlanticbooks.com
E-mail: orders@atlanticbooks.com

Printed & bound in India by Atlantic Print Services

To
Neeraj, my son

and

Anusuya, my daughter

'Shiv Kumar is a gifted poet—poetry is a gift given by the gods.'

Khushwant Singh (*The Tribune*)

'Shiv's best is superb. Poets can learn a lot from him. Poetically, he is the high priest of modernism.'

Keki N. Daruwalla (*The Hindu*)

'...an authentic major voice...in the Indian English poetic milieu.'

(*World Literature Today*)

'The poems are evocative and traverse a highly emotional path looking for some radical meaning in the dreariness of modern life.'

(*Indian Review of Books*)

'...Fascinating...powerful, insightful....'

(*Time Out*, London)

'Kumar's poems emanate from a thought; the epicenter is in the mind.... His words often assume a form bigger than their meaning.'

(*The Journal of the Poetry Society of India*)

'Kumar's poetry is a picture-gallery with deft strokes which, at times, grip the mind of the reader like the tentacles of an octopus.'

(*Poetcrit*)

THE DALAI LAMA

FOREWORD

At my time of life, I have accumulated enough experience to be completely confident that the teachings of the Buddha are both relevant and useful to humanity. If you put them into practice, it is certain that not only you but others too, will benefit. This is surely true of other faiths too, but I have also come to the conclusion that whether or not people are religious believers does not matter much. Far more important is that they be good human beings. That is something that can be achieved through constant familiarity and training with positive states of mind.

Through training, we can change; we can transform ourselves. Within Buddhist practice there are various methods of trying to sustain a calm mind when some disturbing event takes place. Through repeated practice of these methods we can reach a point where a disturbance may occur, but the negative effects on our mind remain on the surface, like the waves that may ripple on the surface of an ocean but don't have much effect deep down. But this is achieved through steady practice; it does not happen overnight.

The *Dhammapada* is a handbook of practical ethics, that may be of interest and benefit, whether you are a Buddhist or not. But more than that, as a collection of verses that consist of statements and advice directly attributed to the Buddha, it represents a succinct summary of the Buddhist path.

Derived from the ancient Pali canon, the *Dhammapada* was not translated into Tibetan until relatively recently. However, another work, the *Udanavarga*, translated from the Sanskrit, contains many corresponding verses and was one of the six primary scriptures of the Kadampa tradition founded in the eleventh century Tibet. The early Kadampa masters adopted an approach to the spiritual life based on an open-minded practice of hearing, contemplation and meditation. This meant that whatever they learned through study, hearing and contemplation was integrated into their mindstreams and, as far as possible, was applied in actual practice.

It is said that bringing about discipline within your mind is the essence of the Buddha's teaching. This is because a disciplined mind leads to happiness and an undisciplined mind leads to suffering. The *Dhammapada*, like the *Udanavarga*, describes a path of ethical behaviour that is a feature of this kind of inner discipline that leads to a happier existence. It includes advice suitable for everyone, whether they are beginners or advanced practitioners of Buddhism or people who simply seek a path to happiness. I offer my prayers that readers who wish to do so will be successful in putting the advice it contains into practice.

The Dalai Lama

Preface

Deeply stuck as we are today in the morass of hatred, anger and violence, the only saviour who can salvage us is Gautam Buddha. What can redeem the ailing humanity is the gospel of love, peace, compassion, forgiveness and understanding.

The *Dhammapada,* a Buddhist scripture, not only reads like the *Gita,* with its emphasis on disinterested action, but it may also be taken as the Buddhist manual on the art of living—or 'as a handbook of practical ethics' (to quote from the Dalai Lama's 'Foreword'). Avoid extremes, says the Buddha. Don't let jealousy or greed taint your soul. Whatever vocation you are engaged in, do your duty truthfully, regardless of any concern for profit or loss. Just as we wouldn't like to be hurt, let us not injure anybody else's feelings.

To the contemporary man who seems to have lapsed into sexual promiscuity, the Buddha warns that carnal desire is man's arch-enemy that leads him downhill to misery and suffering. We should learn to distinguish between transient pleasure and permanent joy and peace.

But, above all, it is Buddha's message of social equality and brotherhood of man that has given hope for salvation to countless downtrodden and depressed humanity. Not by birth but by righteous action can man elevate himself to any level of social status. Even a low caste man can become a Brahmin if he lives a life without blemish. Purity of heart is the only pathway to eternal bliss. What is true Dharma, asks the Buddha time and again. It is meditation, right speech, inner discipline, right action, right perception and dedication to the service of others.

I have also provided a brief life of Gautam Buddha that reads like a scenario—a life of quest and renunciation leading him to supreme enlightenment.

I am very grateful to His Holiness, the Dalai Lama, who was gracious enough to write a Foreword to my book.

Shiv K. Kumar

October, 2008
Hyderabad

Contents

Introduction

What our age—riddled with terror, hatred and violence—needs is a saviour like The Buddha who embodies peace, love, compassion and forgiveness. So forceful was the impact of Buddhism, about six centuries before the birth of Christ, that it created its own school of architecture, sculpture, philosophy—and a distinct pattern of life and culture. In a sense, the Buddha was a creature of the *Zeitgeist,* for within a span of about a hundred years before and after his birth, there was Zoroaster in Persia, Confucius in China and Mahavira in India.

He was born, about 563 BC, to King Suddhodana and Queen Mahamaya of the Sakyas, whose kingdom lay at the foothold of the Himalayas, on the frontier of the present day Nepal.

The chronicles narrate how the Buddha's birth was heralded by a dream his mother had, just a day before she delivered. It was a moonlit night and as she had gone deep into sleep, she dreamt that a six-tuskered elephant, white as a divine cow's milk, entered her womb. As she awoke, she felt her breasts heavy with milk. Her heart was a-flutter with rapture and her eyes were a-glow with divine effulgence. When the king asked his priests to interpret this strange dream, he was told that the child about to be born would either be a king of Kings, or a saviour of humanity, whose divine suzerainty would extend all over Asia.

A few months following the conception, Queen Mahamaya left Kapilavastu, the capital of the Sakya kingdom, to be with her parents in Devadana. En route, she stopped at a park in Lumbini where, sheltered under a bower of flowers and fruits, she gave birth to her divine child. It was the day in early summer when the moon consummates its fullness.

As the news was conveyed to King Suddhodana, he arrived post-haste to see his son. On the child's body, Asita, the king's religious counsellor, saw several auspicious signs. So the priests had rightly predicted that the child was destined to become the Buddha, the enlightened one. Not for him the earth to rule, but the vast empire of human souls.

But when Asita first smiled and then cried, the king felt mystified. Why those conflicting emotions, he wondered. Asita then explained his predicament—that while he felt joyous to see such a divine child, he was also tearful that being an old man, he would not live to bask in the divine sunshine of this little god.

It may be noted here that while the child was named Siddharta ("one whose goal in life has been achieved"), the Buddha ("the awakened one") was a title given to him after he attained enlightenment.

His Early Years

The Buddha's life reads like a multi-splendoured scenario—wisdom, valour, love and renunciation. Even as a child, he dazzled his teachers with his precocity. When, at the age of eight, his religious teacher, Vishwamitra, asked his pupil to write the *Gayatri* mantra, the words flowed from his fingers as if he'd known it already. And when it came to mensuration, Siddharta could count upto a million, without a pause.

"There's nothing to teach him, O King," said Vishwamitra, "he knows it all."

It was not his intellectual prowess that pleased the little prince, but the divine questionings that rose in his mind and heart. Why did a worm eat away a rose-petal, and why did a lizard gobble down an insect, he pondered.

Then one day, as he and his cousin Devadatta were playing together in the garden, they saw a flock of swans flying across the sky. While Siddharta was marvelling at the beauty of these birds, he suddenly saw one of them plummeting down, its wings dropping blood. He then heard a shriek piercing the sky, like a human wail. As the swan fell to the ground, Siddharta ran up to it, put it on his knees and started rubbing its wounded bosom against his cheeks. Then, as he poured some water down its gasping throat, the bird gradually began to quicken into life again. While Siddharta's eyes were moist with compassion and love, Devadatta loomed over him like an evil shadow.

"That bird is mine," Devadatta shouted.

"No, it belongs to the saver, not the killer," replied Siddharta.

That too was the verdict of the wise counsellors before whom the matter was placed for judgement. This incident in the Buddha's life was the first realization of one of the central tenets of his Dharma—pity.

More can be wrought through compassion and understanding than the world dreams of. This truth he learnt when he competed against his rival princes for the hand of Yashodhara, the loveliest maid of Kapilavastu. As was the custom with the warrior clans at that time, each suitor was required to display his valour in diverse forms of martial arts such as archery and horse-riding. After Siddharta excelled his rivals in many tests, he was now confronted with the hardest—to ride Kanaka, a wild stallion that was hot-unbridled, and dark as a raven, with eyes glowing like embers. Its mane looked like a brood of snakes let loose from a snake-charmer's basket. Unbridled and unshod, Kanak was brought into the arena, its nostrils breathing fire.

Each suitor was now required to ride this dreadful animal that threw off its back, one by one, all the aspirants to the hand of Yashodhara—the woman with the eyes of a gazelle, the gait of a peacock and the voice of a nightingale.

When King Suddhodana witnessed the fate of the other princes, his heart sank within him. No, he would not let his only son play with fire. But Siddharta had already paced up to the stallion. First he whispered something into the horse's ears and then he saw his right hand rippling up and down the nape of its neck. It seemed as though two pairs of eyes had melted into a pool of love and understanding. All the stallion's fire was gone. It now just lowered its head and let Siddharta ride it around the arena, triumphantly. Its savageness had been subdued with kindness, its anger with love.

But such were not the victories Siddharta was destined to win in later years. The real battle had to be fought and won within the dark recesses of his soul.

Why did a lizard gobble down an insect, and why did a thorn lurk behind a rose petal?

Although his father was determined to provide him with all the luxuries and comforts of a palace, the young prince's mind often broke loose into questionings about life. There were moments when he sank deep into meditation, under some rose-apple tree.

One day, he decided to steal out of the palace. "How does the world look beyond the palace gates[1]," he asked Channa, his trusted charioteer. "How long shall I remain ensconced within the walls of the palace?"

After a thousand hesitations, in fear and trembling, Channa agreed to let him slip out in the royal chariot, in broad day light. This opened the portals of his mind to a world he had never seen. He now encountered the stark reality of human existence that grinds on relentlessly from one pain to another. As they rode through the market-place, Siddharta's eyes landed on the face of an old man with his hair wizened like dry weeds, hands palsied, cheeks sunken like a pair of deflated bellows, and eyes lustreless.

> "Is that man unwell, Channa?"
> "No, Prince, it's just old age."
> "Will old age get me too? And my Yashodhara?"
> "Yes, O Prince," replied Channa. "Like
> every sapling growing into a tree, and then
> withering away."

This gruesome reality unhinged the young handsome prince; his brow wrinkled and he felt as if some fever was racing in his veins.

Just then hobbled right up to the chariot, a man holding an earthen bowl.

"Alms, O fortunate one!" the man implored.

Channa explained that it was a beggar who lived on doles and often went without food—a mere straw at the mercy of the wind. Again, the prince was lost in thought—how could hunger and royal banquets go together? Here was another question that stirred him into introspection. On another day, he saw a sick man weltering in his own excreta, unable to turn over his side.

Then came the rudest jolt to his unsuspecting heart—a corpse on a bamboo frame, on its way to the crematorium.

"What's that, O Channa?"

"A dead body, dear Prince. They will set it aflame, and immerse its ashes in some holy river. No trace of the body will be left behind, finally."

Siddharta drooped his eyes; his hands quaking, he felt a dark film descending in his eyes.

"You mean I'll also come to this end. My wife and my father...."

"All of us, Siddharta." Channa's voice was a broken reed as he saw the prince caught up in an emotional turmoil. But he continued: "That which is born must die—like the sun at dusk, like the spring fading into autumn...."

"No escape from death, then?" the Prince asked.

"Not even have the sages escaped Yama, the god of Death."

"Enough for today, Channa," the Prince muttered. "Back to the palace!"

Deep into meditation again he went, the deepest he'd ever gone so far. There must be a way out, he said to himself.

For the next few days, he was often seen alone sitting under some tree, utterly oblivious of everything around. Like stinging bees attacking a bare face, he felt besieged by thoughts of sorrow and pain. Bound to the wheel of birth and death was man, but he still pursued his fantasies of lust and greed.

Seeing him lost in thought, day and night, King Suddhodana felt deeply worried. He consulted his ministers, who advised him to do something immediately to pull Siddharta out of his melancholia. What could be more effective than a dose of music and dance in the palace? A night of revelry was, therefore, arranged to entertain the prince with dancing and singing by the kingdom's loveliest girls. They were dressed in translucent garments—alluring with their long tasselled hair, eyes darkened with *surma*, palms dyed in manifold tints. They wore bells on their feet that thumped and jingled on the ground as they swayed their hips—temptation even for the gods to abandon their abode in heaven and partake of this revelry.

While the spectators' eyes were focused on the swinging hips, Siddharta's inner eyes brought him back only the gruesome images he'd seen in the market-place—of the decrepit beggar, the tottering old man and the corpse on its way to the cremation ground. Illusion and reality! the prince said to himself.

The revelry went on long past midnight. When it drew to a close and all the guests had departed, the nautch girls, now jaded and worn out, dozed off on the dance floor, their bodies sprawling all over the place in ungainly postures. To Siddharta, they now looked like corpses, all passion spent.

Utterly disillusioned, he shared with Channa his plan to renounce the life of luxury to fathom the genesis of pain—and see if any release was possible from suffering, or even death.

If the choice was between being and nothingness, he must opt for the former. Of course, he did understand the pangs of separation from his beautiful, young wife and his little son, Rahul, who was soon to become a child forsaken by his father. But if it was all predetermined, should he not leave it all to his destiny? He was now twenty-nine, mature enough to choose between light and darkness, between reality and delusion.

It was a moonlit night, the sky illuminating the streets and houses of Kapilavastu with a myriad stars. When the moment of reckoning arrived, Siddharta stood at the doorstep of his bed-chamber and darted a glance at Yashodara, gone deep in slumber—with her left arm curled round her infant son, and her right hand stretched in vain over her husband's pillow, untouched, for he'd already stolen out of the room. I have visualized this scene in my poem "The Renunciation":

> Midnight. The moon, veiled partially
> by a cloud's hem, is a slice
> of some water-melon.

Through a latticed window, the spring
breeze glides into the bed-chamber,
redolent with the jasmines in the garden below.

On a thistledown bed, she's gone deep
into a dream—an infant's head on her
left breast, her right hand stretched in
vain into the other hemisphere, as he had
slipped off quietly to the door.
A brief pause, as he glances
at his wife and son.

But a voice summons him: "The moment
in your horoscope is irrevocable:"

Beyond the city's bounds, a river awaits
him impatiently. Like a man possessed,
he sleepwalks over its waters, bound
on a remote journey to learn from the
flame's tongue the genesis of pain,
from water that it cannot quench
man's thirst for flesh and land—
that he always aches to decipher
the words on the sand even after the tidal
wave has licked them off.

When he returns, years later,
in a mendicant's robe, holding a brass
bowl, she recognises him, in spite of the
halo's effulgence round his head.
He puts out his bowl: "An offering
of your son, please! For who else would
understand what the Bodhi tree
whispered into my ears?"

She smiles, knowing that he has travelled
through the marine world, nine fathoms
deep—and the space above the stars.
Pain, he has now learnt, is born
in the mother's womb, and ends only
when the ashes are silenced
by a sprinkling of milk.

> This happened, more than two millennia
> ago when sages lived in caves, in
> harmony with the wind, rain, thunder—
> and the beasts.
>
> (From *Thus Spake the Buddha*)

Near the palace gates now waited Channa with Siddharta's favourite horse, Kanthaka, saddled and caparisoned as usual, but not realising that it would be his master's last ride on his back. As they stopped on the outskirts of the city, near a river bank, the prince took off all his jewellery and handed it over to his trusted charioteer, who stood beside him in tears, his head bent, his hands quaking.

"Not an occasion for tears, Channa," said the Prince, almost in a whisper, "but for rejoicing because, rid of the burden of luxury, I now feel very light, almost rejuvenated."

All the world now lay before him to explore as a wandering mendicant, clad in saffron. After donning the new robe of an ascetic, he came to be known as Gautama.

His Wanderings

His first voyage as a seeker of truth was down south, where he hoped to find some spiritual guru. He arrived in the capital of the kingdom of Magadha, Rajagatha (now known as Rajgir). Taken in by a handsome young ascetic, lost in deep meditation under a tree, King Bimbisara approached him for his blessings, only to learn that the mendicant was the former prince from Kapilavastu. But when he offered to share his kingdom with Gautama, he responded: "Not again, O King. Having renounced all worldly glory, I must now keep voyaging towards my destination—truth." But Gautama did promise that after attaining enlightenment, he would certainly stop over in Rajgir for a while.

His first teacher, as Gautama narrates in one of his discourses, was Alara Kalama, a reputed sage. From him he learnt how to achieve the state of total non-being ("the sphere of nothing"—*Akinconnayatana*). But when Gautama attained the state of mystical non-being, he asked his guru: "What next?" and realized that even his teacher had not himself gone any further. Humbly, Kalama acknowledged him as his equal, and let him move on to probe the deeper layers of truth. He understood that his young disciple would not settle for anything less than *nirvana*, the ultimate release from the cycle of birth and death.

The next mentor he adopted was Udaka Ramaputta, whose abode was in Senanigama, a village near Uruvala—an idyllic resort (as he describes it himself)—"a lovely woodland grove, with a calm river flowing closeby." A heavenly place indeed it was for meditation and soul-searching. It was during his six-year stay at Uruvala, that he took a significant step towards self-realization.

In Uruvala, he was joined by five ascetics who practised extreme austerities, inflicting hunger and pain on their bodies.

Gautama describes his experience of self-mortification. So fragile he became once that his fellow ascetics thought him to have become lifeless—his limbs like dead creepers, his buttocks a buffalo's hooves, his cheeks two deep hollows, and his eyes the bottom of a deep, dry well. His skin had shrivelled and become emaciated, like an autumn leaf. Then descended upon him the realization that such mortification was futile. What good was it when the mind went numb and became incapable of any clear perception. So he returned to normal nourishment to be able to continue his spiritual voyage. Disillusioned by his decision to give up the ascetic mode of worship, his five companions forsook him as a renegade. He was now alone in Uruvala, to learn that finally each seeker has to come to terms with life on his own. Strait and lonely is the path to Dharma.

He was now on the last lap of his spiritual journey to Gaya. One morning, as he was immersed in meditation under a peepal tree, a young woman, Sujata, the daughter of a villager, brought him a bowl of milk and rice, which was to be his last meal before he attained Enlightenment. When evening fell, he chose the base of an *assaitha* tree (later called the *bodhi*) and decided to sit there cross-legged, eyes half-closed, till he saw the Divine Light.

It was during that night that he found himself engaged in confrontation with Mara, the Tempter, who was equally determined to ensnare his mind in worldly temptations. Most saviours of mankind have had to confront the devil's ingenious ways of luring them away from the path of righteousness. If Jesus Christ was waylaid by the devil in the desert, St. Anthony too had a narrow escape from the Prince of Darkness. Vulnerability of the human mind to wily tempters forms the theme of T.S. Eliot's play *Murder in the Cathedral*, in which Archbishop Beckett feels tempted to visualise his murder as an avenue to martyrdom, a veiled desire for fame after death.

Mara was perhaps the most ingenious spirit that tried to ambush Gautama, his toughest adversary. While he appeared before Gautama's eyes with a horde of his accomplices, the young mendicant had as his defenders (*paramithias*) only the ten virtues he had learnt during his previous lives—poise, love, perseverance, endeavour, wisdom, renunciation, charity, patience, morality and truth.

Mara's first assault was on Gautama's self mortification. The body, he said, is a divine gift, so why deny it the delicacies of food? The soul cannot sustain itself in a physical vacuum. Then Mara reminded him how he had unwisely renounced his privilege to rule over the Sakya kingdom, denying himself the glories of fame and power. Thereafter, he unleashed his subtlest weapon by reminding Gautama how he had walked away from his warm nuptial bed, and how his beautiful young wife was pining away in loneliness and despair. And what sin had his son, Rahul, committed to be denied parental love? Gross irresponsibility and gross betrayal on his part. Then he pointed toward his hundred daughters who stood behind him, each more alluring than the other—and asked him to choose any of these for his pleasure.

But to all these provocations, Gautama responded with indifference, poise and unflinching determination.

"I know you have come to demolish me with your retinue of followers—lust, greed, indolence, anger, fear and self-glorification. But you will not succeed. So waste not your time, O Dark Spirit." Disgruntled and crestfallen, Mara turned away from the mendicant, followed by his army of evil spirits.

Gradually, during the rest of the night, Gautama's meditation unfolded to him, layer by layer, what he had learnt in his previous lives. One may here aptly quote two lines from Robert Browning's poem "Evelyn Hope":

> Through worlds I shall traverse, not a few.
> Much is to learn, much to forget.

In the early hours of that night, we are told, he recalled the knowledge he had acquired during his past lives, while about midnight he achieved "the superhuman divine vision" (*dibba-cakkhu*), the faculty to visualise the death and rebirth of all living creatures. And, finally, during the wee-hours, he saw before his mind's eye the pageant of the Four Noble Truths and the Eightfold path.

It was a full-moon night in the month of May, with the stars shining in a bright sky. When the dawn broke, its crimson progressively dispelling the darkness, he rose from under the *bodhi* tree, like a phoenix. He was no longer Siddharta or Gautama, but the Buddha, "the awakened one". He could have exclaimed like Archimedes: "Eureka! I've found it!" He felt like a bird released from its cage, into free open air. In his own words, he said (so report the chronicles): "My mind felt liberated, and ignorance was eclipsed by knowledge. I saw divine effulgence all around me." The Buddha was thirty-four when he attained Enlightenment, around 528 BC.

Thereafter, he set out on his travels across the country, preaching his own Dharma. But when he passed through Kapilavastu, his native city burst into excitement. Word went round that the prince who had renounced royal glory was now back as a Bhikshu, robed in saffron. When Yashodhara's maid-servant brought her the news, she chose to wait for him in the palace, although she let her little Rahul meet his father at the city-gate. It was a heart-rending scene when the little boy knelt at the Bhikshu's feet. The Buddha, his heart overflowing with divine joy, raised his son to his feet, took off his royal dress and jewellery, and dressed him in saffron. Thus, Rahul became the first child to be taken into the Buddhist fold.

Then the Buddha entered the palace and climbed up to his wife's chamber. Two pairs of eyes now encountered each other—while Yashodhara's eyes overflowed with tears of unbounded joy, the Bhikshu stood there with a benign smile rippling over his face. She then fell at the feet of her husband, now a blessed saviour of all humanity. King Suddhodana, who was standing closeby, felt deeply touched by his son's homecoming. Then he broke into words:

> "Son, since you were gone, she has remained in a state of mourning. When Channa returned to the palace with your clothes and jewellery, she also took to simple living—sleeping on the floor and eating only once a day."

Overwhelmed by his wife's dedication, he took her also into the Buddhist fold as the first woman monk.

But back he was on the road, as a wandering preacher, determined to bring all men and women within the fold of his new Dharma of truth.

When King Bimbisara of Magadh, one of the Buddha's fervent admirers, learnt that the Master would be passing through his kingdom, he ordered fancy brass lamps to be put up in his honour all along the streets. The King of Divine Light must be received with illuminations everywhere, he proclaimed.

In his capital, there lived a poor, old woman who worshipped the Buddha with all her mind and soul. With no money to buy a brass lamp, she tore a piece of cloth from her tattered sari, rolled it into a wick and held in her hand an earthen lamp with a little mustard oil in it. Thus, she waited at the doorstep of her cottage for the Master to pass by.

Unfortunately for the King, when the illustrious visitor entered the town, a roaring wind rose and extinguished all the brass lamps. There now remained only a solitary earthen lamp in the capital to greet the Buddha, its feeble flame protected by this old woman's wrinkled palm. When the Buddha passed by her cottage, she knelt at the Master's feet, and asked for his blessings, holding her tiny earthen lamp, still a-flutter. So deeply moved was the Buddha by the woman's devotion and love that he turned to his disciples and said, "There, you see this votary whose earthen lamp will illuminate the world when all other lights go out. It is not gold or brass that enriches the soul, only unflinching faith."

Death came to the Buddha when he was eighty. For quite some time, he had been ailing. He had even told his followers, particularly Ananda, his closest disciple, that he had only a few months ahead of him. When he arrived at Pava, a village near Vaisali, a city he had visited several times, he accepted the invitation of Cunda, a goldsmith, to have a meal at his house, together with his other Bhikshus. But, as if he had divined his end, he asked his host not to serve the same food to his Bhikshus. As soon as he finished eating, he felt sickness creeping through his limbs. Buddhist scholars have offered diverse interpretations of the last meal he had at Vaisali. Was it pork, or a kind of mushroom found in a spot trodden by pigs? But whatever was the food, it brought him close to death. It was as though, like Jesus Christ, he had just finished his last supper. When Ananda saw his master in a death agony, he started to cry. But the Buddha consoled him:

> "No, Ananda, thou shalt not grieve. Remember that anything that is born must perish. That is the stark reality. What remains after the extinction of the body is a man's deeds." To his other Bhikshus, he said: "Your real Master hereafter should be the Dharma, not the body that was Gautama."

He breathed his last in the month of May, the month that had brought him the Enlightenment. The wheel had come full circle and it was time to depart.

Death is a recurrent theme in the *Dhammapada*, as an inevitable finalé to every birth. There is an interesting incident in the Buddha's life that illustrates his dramatic mode of reminding his followers that there is no escape from death. Once, in the course of his wanderings, a woman named Krishna Gautami, saw him meditating under a tree. Taken in by the divine glow on his face, she approached him for a boon. Could he invoke his divinity to salvage her only son from a deadly disease?

"Indeed I can, sister," responded the Buddha, "if you'd only bring me a handful of mustard seed from anyone. But," he paused to add, "only from a house that has never encountered death."

So went the woman on her rounds, from house to house, asking for a handful of mustard seed. But while everyone was only too willing to give her any quantity of mustard seed, none could fulfil the second condition. Because death had visited every house.

"So, sister," he said "you must learn to endure the inevitable."

In one of his discourses, the Buddha exhorts every Bhikshu to keep the sails of his soul's boat prim and unfurled, for one may have to set out for the last journey, anytime.

His Teaching

The essence of the Buddha's teaching is capsuled in the Four Noble Truths and the Eightfold path. If these Truths constitute the divine precepts, the Eightfold path shows all humans the way to righteous action. Each of these truths is based on the Master's personal experience. This is what makes Buddhism also a pragmatic way of life.

The Four Noble Truths

The First Truth is a statement of the fact that suffering is an inalienable coordinate of human existence. A babe's first cry at birth symbolises his initiation into pain that will accompany it until the last moment. This truth is also articulated in a couplet by Mirza Ghalib, the celebrated Urdu poet:

Qaid-é hayat o bundé ghum
asl mein donon ek hain

Maut se pehlé aadmi
ghum se nijat paye kyun.

Bondage of existence and the
bondage of pain are coterminous.

How can man expect release from
suffering till his last breath?

But if suffering accompanies man ceaselessly all through his voyage of life, it also awakens him to self-realization. "Where there is suffering there is holy ground," is the opening sentence in Oscar Wilde's *De Profundis*.

All humans, the Buddha tells us, desire peace and prosperity—a happily married life, health, success and fame. And yet what they invariably experience is tension and deprivation, disease and failure. This is because human life is crushed under the grinding wheel of change, and change is what can never bring one happiness. So every man is caught in this flux, like a spider in its own web.

The Second Truth enlightens us to the genesis of pain, the cause that engenders anguish. That cause, we should understand, lies in our insatiable desires, our pursuit of material achievement. Like a moth longing to be a star and the night yearning for the morrow, man always chases his fantasies—money, power and lust. All mortals are caught in this rat race, each jostling against the other, mindlessly. So the real culprit is our selfish desire, a fire that keeps raging within us all the time. Not all the oceans in the world can extinguish it and not all our pious resolutions. If one desire is muzzled for a while, another rears up its ugly head, stoking up the blood in our veins, ceaselessly.

Now let us understand the Third Noble Truth which explains the relationship between cause and effect. If a man could diagnose his ailment correctly, he would be able to find a cure for it. Wouldn't it be a disaster if a physician tried his medication for loss of hair and appetite when his patient was actually suffering from cancer? So, a man could attain *nirvana* only if he pulled out the roots of his suffering—his selfish desires.

The only hope for a human being is the Buddha's Fourth Noble Truth, the Eightfold Path which is the sole avenue to achieve eternal peace through release from the bondage of birth and death. This truth is like a divine wheel, with eight spokes, that carries one forward to *nirvana*.

Right comprehension is the first spoke of this wheel, one of the cardinal tenets of the Dharma. It is only through correct understanding that one can realise true peace which does not come from outside, but from within oneself. Divine light is already there inside one's soul. Right comprehension alone will enable a man to sift the chaff from the wheat, the outer crust from the seed underneath, the shadow from the reality and the transient from the perennial. It is, therefore, essential that a man nurtures discrimination to achieve spiritual advancement.

From right comprehension flows right purpose which is the faculty to identify one's real goal in life. Out of sloth and indifference a man may drift in life, like a dead branch tossed about on the surface of a river. No forward movement in life is possible without a clear sense of purpose, which is like a compass in the hands of a navigator. Right purpose, therefore, alone opens the portal to wisdom.

Right speech is the third spoke in the wheel of the Dharma. Tender speech adds to the flavour of human existence. While an abrasive tongue wounds like a sabre, a word softly spoken acts like a balm. The Buddha himself always addressed his disciples gently and affectionately, as his "brothers and sisters" to let them all feel as his equals. Tender speech is a mark of humility, of oneness with all other living creatures.

If a man speaks righteously, he will never lapse into lying which is the obverse of truth. Dissimulation and prevarication are the ugly faces of falsehood. Righteousness alone can make a man speak out boldly in defence of his virtuous actions.

Closely linked to right speech is right conduct, for a man is really known by his action and demeanour. This is because someone may speak tenderly, articulate noble truths and yet act deviously and ignobly. *Nirvana* is not attained through noble words spoken but only by virtuous deeds done.

This leads to the next step towards self-realization—right occupation. How can a man engage himself in an unworthy profession and still achieve inner peace? Into this category fall thieves who operate in the darkness of night; butchers, who slice up birds and animals, and soldiers who are trained only to kill. If the Buddha had been alive today, he would have denounced all nuclear scientists as evil creatures, engaged in making weapons of mass destruction at the behest of their warlords. Far more blessed is a farmer who ploughs his field in summer or winter to grow food for his fellow human beings. The choice of right occupation is, therefore, a man's prime pathway to divine life.

Right endeavour, the next spoke in the Divine Wheel, is vitally instrumental in enabling a man to achieve his goal. It is like a man climbing up a ladder step by step, or like a bullock pulling its cart steadfastly, or a trained race-horse that must overcome all obstacles on the track, mindful only of its goal. If a man's will sags as he is climbing up a hill, he is certainly doomed to slide downward. So let not a man loosen his hold on life. Tireless effort and single-mindedness are the cornerstones of our success in life.

The next step in a seeker's quest for truth is right attention. Nothing worthwhile can be attained without absolute concentration in whatever one undertakes to do. Whether a man is a poet, a sage, a navigator or an archer, he must not let his mind wander. This is how Dronacharya taught archery to the young Pandava and Kaurava princes, in the *Mahabharata*. When in the course of training he asked his pupils to tell him how they would shoot a bird hidden somewhere in the foliage of a tree, diverse came the responses. If one prince saw only the branch of the tree on which perched the bird, the other could identify the bird itself. But Arjuna replied that he could see neither the branch, nor the bird, but only a pair of eyes glistening in the tree. That's how he won his guru's prophesy that he would someday shape into the mightiest archer of his time. The only way to hit the bull's eye is to control one's attention, bring the eye and the hand in perfect harmony before letting the arrow fly out.

But, above all, it is right meditation that is a man's prime asset, for it is the most effective instrument in controlling one's mind that leaps like a monkey from one tree-top to another, always looking for fruits. Only when it is collared and disciplined by its trainer can it be made to perform at the master's will.

This stresses the primacy of the last spoke in the wheel of the Eightfold Path—meditation which alone can enable a man to tame the mind's vagrancy. Buddhism, therefore, has evolved an elaborate system of meditation, offering man his release from misery (*dukha*).

But before one can descend into the deep well of introspection, it is necessary that one should empty one's mind of the lumber of all worldly embroilments. It is like cleaning a vessel before it is ready for cooking. This is itself a very difficult operation because the mind would resist withdrawing itself from thoughts of profit, passion or self-glory. But unless the mind's slate is completely wiped off, it will not be ready for fresh writing.

This entails determination, perseverance and, above all, absolute concentration. An apt illustration to understand this is the experiment in physics of removing the parallax. The experimenter is required, through careful adjustment of his instruments, to reach a point where he sees an object near his eyes, another at some distance, and also an object in infinity, till all the three move on the same plane as if merged into a state of harmony.

While a man needs an ingeniously designed spacecraft to land on the moon or Mars, he can set out to explore the inner spaces of his being without the assistance of any external apparatus. He has just to close his eyes to his environment and descend into the depths of his soul, like a diver who gets to the bottom of a pool.

This may explain why the Buddha attaches great importance to meditation (*Dhyana*), which alone acts as a medium of self-purification and spiritual enlightenment. But it is an operation that draws upon a man's ultimate resources, both mental and physical. In this context, one may recall the traditional image of the Buddha seated cross-legged, with both eyes closed, focused only on the epicentre of his inner being.

Four Levels of Meditation

To reach the fourth and final stage of meditation, which brought the Buddha his enlightenment, one has to pass through three intermediary stages, each highly formidable and exacting. It is like a pyramid with a triangular base, tapering off to the top—the pinnacle of divine bliss.

First Level of Meditation

This constitutes the first rung of the ladder leading to the top. It is like one's initiation into exploring a brave, new world of divine rapture that surpasses all earthly pleasures.

When we are viewing an engaging serial on the TV, listening to a symphony, or watching a ballet, we remain absorbed in rapt attention, lost to all other sensory sensations. We are then transported to another world, away from everyday life. This is precisely the kind of experience we get when we move into meditation, withdrawing our consciousness from all sounds and sights around us. It is like moving into a sort of spiritual Walt-Disney land with its own wonders—released from the grey dailiness of life. Aptly, the Buddha calls it "right attention," which is a state of mystical oneness with the inner spirit. Sounds from the outside world then seem to come from another hemisphere. We feel as if some power has disconnected our being from the outside world. When we come out of such a state, we feel like a movie-goer who emerges from the cinema-hall, dazzled and disturbed by the lights and faces outside, because his mind is still held by the images he had seen on the screen.

At this level, the meditator becomes subliminally conscious of the working of his own mind which, unhinged from its customary attachments, now sees itself floating in a void, eager to find a prop or a foothold. Used to wandering listlessly in the work-a-day world, the mind finds it difficult to turn inwards, like a driver who struggles to reverse his vehicle in a narrow lane.

Ordinarily, the mind swings like a pendulum, from stimulus to response, from one emotion to another, along a chain of associations. In this preliminary stage of meditation, the mind must learn to subjugate all personal emotions of love and hate, likes and dislikes. Until it is rid of all attachments, it will not be ready for the next phase of its spiritual voyage.

Since this is only the first lap of a long, arduous journey, a man should not expect any spurts of spiritual illumination, any epiphanies. Let him be just consoled by the fact that a foundation has been laid for a four-storey building to come up in due course. But let him also remember that only those who reach the fourth stage of meditation will achieve enlightenment.

Second Level of Meditation

Any discussion about the different levels of meditation is erroneous because, in the grey regions of the mind, there are no well-charted borderlines. It is just one diffused mass of mental activity in which one level of operation often overlaps the other. But since clarity has its own compulsions, an effort is being made here to suggest different degrees of intensity in the course of meditation.

So, admitting certain infirmities in this logical analysis, let us now try to unravel the mystery of the second phase of *Dhyana*. While the first level of meditation pertains to a man's unconscious self—his urges, thoughts, emotions and temperament—in the second phase, his concentration becomes denser, for his mind is now able to probe the deeper layers of his subliminal self. If the outside sensory sensations are still heard knocking at the door of one's consciousness, this noise has now become muted. No longer do the woodpeckers of the outer self sound as shrill as in the initial stage. It is as though the mind now feels confident enough to win a battle for domination over one's desires which no longer come disguised as tempters, but in their real forms. Our ego no longer flexes its muscle because its "I-ness" and "Mine-ness" are gone.

The mind now snaps its immediate relationships—bonds between father and son, husband and wife, sister and brother. On the other hand, it enlarges the scope of its compass to include all other selves. In this widening of relationships, there is no demarcation even between friends and enemies. This perception of universal fellowship lies at the heart of Buddhism which recognises no barriers of caste, colour, creed or sex. The walls of separateness are now demolished and the entire world emerges as one large, cohesive family.

The conquest of one's insurgent desires is indeed a painful operation, but finally it brings in its wake an upsurge of joy and peace. Like a mother feeling light and buoyant after delivering her child at the end of her labour pains.

As one descends into the deeper recesses of one's mind, one feels like a frogman who floats far below the surface of water to identify what lies hidden at the sea's bottom—beyond the ken of those who stand on the shore, burdened by their consciousness.

At this stage, the mind does not run at full speed, propelled by compulsive urges, but moves at a snail's pace, like a cinema-projector showing images in slow motion. Thought is no longer a continuum, but it flashes out in segments as separate entities. In this lax movement of the mind, one may even be able to visualise each thought marching past like a soldier, in a single line. At this slow pace, the mind gathers more energy, like a man whose blood pressure slides down during his hours of sleep.

It is not easy to understand this extraordinary change in the mental process; in fact, this development is one of the most elusive concepts of Buddhism. This is something that can only be experienced, not rationally understood, because it is identical with a mystical feeling that defies any logical reasoning.

What is implicit here is the prime importance of tranquillity, because anything perceived in a state of tension becomes distorted. It is only a calm and poised mind that can perceive objects in their correct perspective. Viewed through the prism of meditation, therefore, life acquires a new coherence and meaning. How can the observer of a painting in a museum appreciate it fully if he stands too close to it? Just as it is distance that lends perspective to the eye, so does meditation enable the mind to assess every experience dispassionately.

The Third Level of Meditation

If the chain of thoughts has been broken, one may as well ask: is there anything that intervenes between one thought and another? The answer lies in the fact that in the first instance consciousness cannot be visualized as a chain, because it is like a ripple in the pool of our thought-process. So between one thought and another, the mind only stands still and poised as if held on the crest of an upsurge of ecstasy.

According to the Buddha, when the thought-process diminishes to a trickle, the mind reaches a point where the sequence of thoughts comes to a standstill and the meditator catches a glimpse of his consciousness. With a burst of spiritual effulgence it arrives, lighting up all the dark niches of the self.

This state, like beatitude, has been called *bodhi*, or supreme awareness.

This marks the transition from the second to the third level of meditation. Anyone who crosses this seemingly insuperable barrier is already on his way to enlightenment. It is, to use the Buddha's favourite metaphor, like crossing a river from one bank to the other. To savour this experience a man has to take off his old mental garments—the conglomeration of his greed, anger and lust—before diving into the cool, dark waters of the blissful unconscious.

The Fourth Level of Meditation

Arriving at the fourth stage of *Dhyana* is like passing through the swinging portals of a mansion to find oneself suddenly in front of a door that opens into the treasure-house of spiritual bliss. But entry through this door is possible only for the man who is capable of infinite patience, unflinching dedication and a will to transcend his worldly desires.

It should be remembered that even if a man has successfully crossed the first three stages, his mind may still be assailed in its unguarded moments by his passions which lie dormant but not entirely vanquished. So let him not loosen his hold on the mind and walk through life like an unwary traveller. He should never forsake awareness and vigilance—a man's priceless props.

In the subliminal zones of the unconscious, determination loses its potency. Still, even in this uncharted region, a man must grope his way toward Dharma, guided by his instinct if not will-power. Let the seeker not forget that his ultimate destination is *nirvana*, release from the bondage of birth and death. So to achieve this, he must establish harmony with all living creatures, for while separation is debasing, unity is divine. At this stage, all barriers crumble down and one sees only one vast landscape of humanity. When a man emerges from this final stage, he may still be dimly aware of his old identity, but he will now walk about the world as an awakened man, like a phoenix risen from the ashes.

It was after this awakening within himself, that the Buddha rose from under the *bodhi* tree, a man anointed with divinity—

a man whose voice sounded above the winds. No longer was for him the cycle of birth and death.

As he says in the **Dhammapada**:

Many a mansion have I lived in,
seeking him who fabricated this

prison of senses, steeped in sorrow.
Such was my endless struggle!

But, O architect of this mud-house,
now that I have seen thee, never

again, shall I let you build these walls
of suffering, nor nurture this lofty

tree of falsehood, nor raise new columns
on this clay. Demolished is this

house, its columns fractured—all
designed by deception! Now I

shall voyage forward to my ultimate
goal—nirvana!

The Dhammapada

Chapter One

Commentary

What singles out the **Dhammapada** from many other scriptures is the poetic mode in which it conveys its message to us—in a language that is simple and forthright.

The opening chapter sets the tone of the entire scripture—its emphasis on the supremacy of the mind over the body, for it is our thoughts that mould our existence. We are what we think. Little do most humans realize that life is too brief to be squandered away in imagining how other people may be conspiring to harm us. Such thoughts only impoverish the soul. It is not anger or retaliation that can control an explosive situation—only love, compassion and understanding.

It is our wanton pursuit of pleasure that makes us vulnerable to Mara, the Tempter. It is our selfishness that keeps us enmeshed in pain, both during our brief sojourn on this earth and the life hereafter. So let every man engage himself in thoughts that are lofty and spiritual and practise what he may have learnt from the scriptures. For it is not the saffron robe that shows a virtuous man but his inner purity and self-discipline.

DOUBLE-LAYERED VERSES

A man's thoughts always hover over his head, each prodding him to action. If pain follows an evil thought, like the wheels of a bullock cart, a chaste thought accompanies him like a shadow. A man is moulded by his mind—he is what he thinks.

A host of phantoms waylays a common man everywhere. "That man has hurled a stone of anger at me; this one has assaulted me." This is how we always remain caught in the snare of anger and hatred.

But he who lets not such thoughts keep buzzing around his ears, shall be rid of wrath and ill-will. Because hatred begets animosity, binding a man to an endless chain of contempt—while love, an immutable law of life, generates peace and joy.

Let a man always remember that human existence is like a passing cloud that relieves him from the sun's heat but for just a short while. Then will he be released from all the tensions of life, forever.

Just as a powerful wind uproots a fragile tree, so does Mara, the Tempter, ambush a feeble mind. Never will a man be at peace with himself if he indulges in fancies of earthly pleasures—eats too much, toiling too little and always at the mercy of his carnal desires.

He who dresses himself in saffron without first cleansing his mind, is not worthy of this colour. Also, he who is devoid of tranquillity and self-discipline, does not deserve to be robed in saffron. But he whose mind is chaste like lustral water, may dress himself thus, for it is the colour of a man's thoughts that really shows him.

A man who falls a prey to delusions and lends himself to trivialities, is like a straw at the mercy of an idle wind. Vainly may such a man chase fame and wealth, but he will be denied the light of wisdom. On the other hand, he who can tell

a vain muttering from a holy chant,
a kernel from its husk,
an illusion from reality
has realized the truth.

Rain water may trickle down the roof of a hut, but even a heavy downpour cannot sweep a well-disciplined mind off its poise and serenity—unassailable as it is by rain, thunder or storm.

Suffering in this life and hereafter will be the lot of every human being whose thoughts always eddy around his own self. He will reap only a bitter fruit for his selfish actions. But he who transcends his self, always letting his hands reach out to others, in love and compassion, will savour peace and joy, here and hereafter—for the good deeds he has done during his brief sojourn on this earth.

But no refuge is possible for those who remain imprisoned within the four walls of their selves—like a small animal hiding itself in a hole. Pain is for them during this existence and more suffering awaits them in the life hereafter.

He who can chant mantras from the scriptures, engage himself in rituals, but has not moulded his actions to Dharma, is like a cowherd who wastes his time counting somebody else's cows. Not for him is there any solace or peace amidst life's pain, both mental and physical.

However, he whose scriptural knowledge is limited, but who has controlled the wild beasts of hatred, carnal desire and self-delusion, shall attain divine wisdom. Such a man walks through life steadfastly—in sun and shade, in joy and sorrow.

Chapter Two

Commentary

The Buddha's message is invariably pragmatic in exhorting man to be always aware of himself and the world around him. Ceaseless vigilance—that is the key to *nirvana*, escape from birth and death.

Meditation is a form of inner awakening, a cleansing process that leads one to a life of pure thought and deed. A man who is ever vigilant will never lapse into indolence or lust. He always keeps his eyes open, while others around him are lost in unawareness.

A man who is committed to spiritual pursuits, who is always earnest and active, will be able to liberate himself from all the shackles of senses. He alone will savour the highest state of bliss—*nirvana*.

VIGILANCE

Always remain vigilant while crossing the borderline of life. If you are not ever-watchful, you'll not escape Yama, the god of Death. He who endeavours whole-heartedly will vanquish him, but he whose determination sags will never attain eternal life. A wise man can unveil this mystery; he feels happy sharing with others his enlightened thoughts. If you descend into the cool, deep cave of meditation and not let your spirit slacken, you will savour eternal peace and bliss.

Divine grace will keep you under its wings if you remain engaged in noble actions, with a heart pure and well-disciplined, in harmony with the law of Dharma—truth. You will then find yourself in the haven of an island that no tempest or strong wind can overwhelm. Your life will be like an oasis in a vast wilderness.

While the uninitiated and feeble-minded lose their hold on vigilance, the sagacious ones treasure it like a rare pearl in a shell. Let not indolence and lust waylay you on your life's journey. That way lies disaster. Let your meditation lead you like starlight through a dark forest—from pain to divine joy.

A man who shakes off indolence, like a snake sloughing off its old skin, will rise from the valley of suffering to the hilltop of happiness and knowledge. Like an eagle, he will view a plain from its nest atop a hill. Such a man will salvage himself from the pain and suffering of those who are embroiled in worldly pursuits.

Those who rise from the depths of sloth, can awaken others who are still lost in slumber. The enlightened ones go leaping forward like a race horse, leaving behind others in the dust. It was through persistent endeavour that Indra rose to be the Chief of gods. While the earnest ones command veneration from the others, the slothful are ignored by everyone.

Like a flame, the spiritually awakened man forges ahead, shaking off his worldly chains. He has gone the way of no return—to *nirvana.*

Chapter Three

Commentary

Here the Buddha emphasises the imperative need to subjugate one's mind, like a skilled archer who trains his arrow at the bull's eye. A formidable task it certainly is, but it is the only way to overcome suffering.

A vagrant mind is like a straw in an idle wind, at the mercy of every transient desire. But the enlightened one is able to break a wandering mind into discipline, by channelling its thoughts in the right direction. That is the way to peace, health and joy.

The Buddha reminds man, again and again, that the body is a feeble mud-house, prone to decay and extinction. But one can transform it into an impregnable fort, through self-control.

So also, says Guru Nanak,—it is the mind that is both the vanquisher and the vanquished, the master and the slave.

MIND

As a skilled archer aims his arrow at the bull's eye, so does the enlightened one bring to focus his restless and vagrant mind—a task formidable indeed, well-nigh impossible.

As a fish angled and abandoned on the sandy beach, writhes in agony, fluttering and gasping for breath, so does the mind just initiated into meditation, is eager to dodge Mara, the sly Tempter.

Difficult it is to control one's mind that leaps like a monkey from one housetop to another. But a mind broken into discipline, like a colt trained by its master, attains health, both spiritual and physical. Such a strong-minded man escapes the clutches of Mara.

Unwise are those
  who let their thoughts flit about like
    autumn leaves in the wind and
  who are indifferent to Dharma, the
    central prop of life.
But the enlightened ones are those
  whose thoughts run a steady course,
    like a boat sailing smoothly
  whose minds are ever poised and
    serene, transcending all
    opposites—good or bad
  whose minds are ever vigilant, rid
    of fear or anxiety.

One should never forget that the human body is a weak clay-pot, prone to decay and destruction. A fragile mud-house it is that cannot withstand wind or rain. So let your mind be a strong fortress with granite walls, lofty towers and ramparts—to fight and vanquish Mara with the sword of wisdom. Do not ever forget that a man's body will soon go mute like a log of wood which will be burnt to ashes—a handful of dust, valueless.

More injurious to a man is his own vagrant mind than the harm done to him by his foes. A mind ever poised yields greater good to a man than anything that comes to him from his mother, father, family or friends.

Chapter Four

Commentary

The Buddha is essentially a poet whose discourses are replete with metaphors, similes and images. This makes his teachings both visual and dramatic.

In this chapter, flowers are used as an expanded metaphor. Like a skilled florist who knits flowers of diverse hues and aroma into a garland, so does an enlightened man chooses the right path of Dharma to attain *nirvana*.

Flowers are multifaceted symbols. When Mara uses his flower-tipped arrows to ambush an unwary person into lust and death, they symbolise a man's futile quest for sensory pleasures. So why squander away one's life gathering flowers?

A man will be like a flower, with both colour and aroma, if he translates into action what he has learnt from his teachers. He will not be like a flower with bright colour but no fragrance—all words but no deeds.

What is central to the Buddha's teaching is his stress on practice, not precept. Since knowledge alone cannot carry a man very far, he must also pattern his life according to his ideals. That is where the human will often falters. To quote from John Drinkwater's poem "Prayer":

> Give us the will to fashion as we feel,
>
> Grant us the strength to labour as we know,
>
> Grant us the purpose, ribbed and edged with
> steel,

To strike the blow...

Give us courage to build above the deep intent
The deed, the deed!

FLOWERS

As a florist knits into a garland flowers of proper hue, fragrance and size, so should a man choose the right road to Dharma, which will help him transcend the bounds of death—and attain *nirvana*.

If you always remember that the body is transient like a bubble, a mirage in a desert, you'd be able to withstand the flower-embedded arrows of Mara. Then death will have no dominion over you.

Just as an incensed flood inundates a village immersed in slumber, so does Death wash away all those who waste their lives picking flowers—enmeshed in playful pursuits. But to the enlightened, plucking a flower is like decapitating it, dismembering its limbs. So one should act like a bee that flits from flower to flower, savouring honey but without hurting any flower.

Let it not be your concern to judge what the others do or fail to accomplish. Confine your attention to what you do or have failed to achieve.

Those who do not translate into action what they preach to others, are like flowers that carry colour but no fragrance. They are like words that carry sound, but no meaning. But those who practise what they preach are like flowers redolent with both hue and aroma.

Just as a florist can knit a garland from a mass of flowers, so can many virtuous deeds be accomplished in the course of one's life span.

Remember that while the fragrance of sandalwood or flowers cannot go against the wind, that of a noble deed can travel in all directions. Neither the rose nor the jasmine, nor the sandalwood can ever match the aroma released in the air by a righteous action.

Feeble is the fragrance of a rose or sandalwood but not that of a noble deed that rises high to reach even the abode of gods.

The wise, the virtuous and the earnest need never be scared of Mara.

A true votary of the Buddha shines like a star in the heaven, like a flower that rears up its crest out of a heap of waste-matter by the roadside, to delight the eye of every passerby.

Chapter Five

Commentary

A little learning is a dang'rous thing;
Drink deep, or taste not the Pierian spring;
These shallow draughts intoxicate the brain;
And drinking largely sobers us again.

The above lines from Alexander Pope's poem "Essay on Criticism" sum up incisively the nature of an amateur person. Such a man always parades his half-baked knowledge only to expose his hollowness. While there is still some hope for someone who knows his limitations, utterly foolish is he who lacks self-knowledge. Such a man is an enemy to himself. He fantasises that his selfish actions will bear him sweet fruits, but he is disillusioned when he reaps only a bitter harvest.

On the other hand, a wise man, dedicated to selfless deeds, prefers to go his solitary way where there are no fellow travellers.

An unwise monk, according to the Buddha, is one who hankers after false honour, claiming preference over other monks and seeking adulation from everybody around. Such vanity is the undoing of a Bhikshu. Arrogance and carnal desire are a man's prime failings. The golden path to *nirvana* is renunciation of our craving for gain and sensual pleasure.

NOT YET RIPENED

Prolonged is the night of the man who is
not fully awake,
Agonising is the journey of the man who
feels exhausted, and

Endless is the cycle of birth and death
for the man who knows not the laws
of the Dharma.

Be a loner if you have no companion to
share the travails of your spiritual
journey.

Lean not for support on the immature who
say to themselves:
"These children are mine,
And so is this wealth."
But can they even take themselves as
their own, not to speak of their family
or possessions?

Some redemption is still possible for those
who are aware of their failings.
They may still claim a modicum of wisdom.

But utterly vain and foolish are those
who parade themselves as enlightened.

Not for them the light of Dharma, even
if they spend their entire life in the
company of the wise. For can a
spoon relish the taste of soup? Nor
can a jewel-box understand the
value of the rubies and diamonds
inside it.

If only an immature person could live for
a short while with the enlightened,
he would then comprehend Dharma.
Like the tongue that tastes the soup.

Those who are not yet fully ripened turn
out to be their own enemies. They
reap only suffering for their selfish
actions. So why engage oneself in
a deed that leads only to repentance
and pain?

But virtuous is the deed that brings in its
wake only joy, not repentance. Such
an action is selfless. Like the bee that
collects honey only for the others.

To the selfish man, his actions taste sweet,
till he finds them turn sour, finally.
What follows then is only suffering.

Therefore, even if a man fasts
for weeks and months, he will
not be able to realize the happiness
of the man who has comprehended
Dharma.

Just as a bowl of milk requires some time to freeze into curd, so does a selfish action need a short while to result in pain and suffering. Like a cub that takes a little time to let its paws grow into talons, spiked and lethal. Like embers that smoulder under the ash only to erupt into flames to engulf the uninitiated man who gathers a smattering of knowledge—only to be misused, not harnessed beneficially. Such a Bhikshu longs for vain glory—for preference over fellow monks and for recognition from everyone. He says:

> "Lend me your ears, O monks and householders. I have the power to do anything. All my actions are proper, while yours are wrong."

Thus, he falls a prey to his ego, his arrogance and passion.

So, O votaries of the Buddha, lend not your minds and hearts to pride and to gain worldly happiness. But keep walking steadily on the path that will take you to *nirvana*. Like a pilgrim who trudges slowly but steadily up the hill to the peak of divine bliss. Let wisdom be your goal and Dharma your destination.

Chapter Six

Commentary

The role of a wise guru in life has always been considered paramount in the East. So if a man is fortunate enough to find a true guide, he should both revere and obey him. Let your guru admonish you or censure you, for his aim is only to guide you through the maze of life.

A wise man does not indulge in speaking vainly or idly. Nor is he led by any desire for money, position or fame. His only aim is to live in accordance with the dictates of the Dharma so that he may be prepared to face death anytime.

In the **Dhammapada**, the metaphor of the river occurs frequently—the river of life on the other shore of which abides eternal bliss, freedom from suffering and death. But this is possible only if one follows the path of renunciation—of disengagement from all worldly attachments.

THE SAGACIOUS

If you encounter a man, wise and pious, who takes you away from the path of evil, let him lead you. For he will be your pole-star, your lamp that will help you negotiate a sharp bend in a dark forest. Such a man will guide you to the secret divine treasure—of peace and bliss.

Let such a man be your friend and pathfinder. You should even encourage him to censure you if you stumble into the wrong path. Let him caution you against succumbing to temptation. Such a man will be adored by the virtuous and shunned by the evil-minded.

Always seek the company of the sagacious, truthful and virtuous. Follow not those who are tainted, both in word and deed. Be like the sunflower that turns only to the sun's visage.

As the sagacious are like torch-bearers to ordinary men, follow the path of Dharma as shown by them. They will teach you how to live joyously, with mind sombre and balanced.

Just as a navigator leads water to any desired place, an archer trains his arrow at the bull's eye and a carpenter chisels wood into any shape, so does an enlightened man mould an ordinary person's mind into nobility.

Just as even a powerful wind cannot shake a massive boulder, so too neither censure nor praise shake a sagacious man. When a man listens to the voice of Dharma, his mind grows tranquil and lucid like a lake unruffled by the wind.

A virtuous man keeps walking forward, regardless of whatever happens during his journey. He does not indulge in idle speech and keeps himself equidistant from good or evil, friend or foe. You will recognise a man as enlightened if he does not yearn to acquire money, status, family or success, through means fair or foul.

While most humans remain embroiled in their worldly pursuits on this side of the river of life, only a few reach the other shore where abide eternal peace and joy. Only the boat of Dharma will ferry you across this river—Dharma that will help you vanquish even death.

He who makes it to the other shore is rid of this world's darkness—he sees light on the other side. Such a man, well-versed in the multiple zones or enlightenment, renounces his family, snaps all ties with worldly attachments, subjugates his senses, to enjoy true liberation from pain. He walks alone, robed in the light of truth.

Chapter Seven

Commentary

The Buddha's concept of wisdom and sainthood is the same. The saint, according to him, is one who walks through life unburdened of all desires, in peace and freedom—like a wayfarer who is not attracted by any object or person on the way. An Urdu verse conveys the same idea thus:

Bazar sé guzra hoon

kharidar nahin hoon.

I am just a passerby in this market place,

without any desire to buy anything.

Like nomads, saints wander from place to place. They sanctify any place they choose to abide for a while. What sustains them in life is meagre food and thoughts that are lofty and noble. Blessed, they can withstand all temptations. Death loses its sting for them, for they have attained *nirvana.*

THE SAGE

A saint is one
who has reached his journey's end,
who has shaken off all shackles, and
who abides in peace and freedom.

A sagacious man is always seeking and
striving; he has no permanent home. He is
like a swan that abandons its lake to
enjoy the freedom of the air.

It is difficult to be on the trail of the selfless,
because they are like a drove of birds always

up on the wings. Free they are, because
they have renounced all worldly
belongings, sustaining themselves
only on alms and meagre food. They
alone are privileged to taste true
freedom because they have muzzled
the wild beasts of their senses.

Such blessed humans are envied even by the gods, because like skilled riders they have reined in their ego and pride. Enduring like the earth, firm like a threshold, unblemished like a lake that is still and mudless, they have transcended birth and death.

Like smouldering embers subsided by a sprinkling of water, their minds are quiescent because peace has blessed their speech, actions and thoughts. Liberated from all personal bonds, illusions and desires, they can envision reality beyond the veil of appearance. They have indeed attained eternal bliss.

Such saints sanctify whatever place they live in—a village, a town, a cottage atop a hill, or a hut deep in a valley. With their passions controlled, their hearts brimful with peace and joy, they exude holiness all around.

Chapter Eight

Commentary

William Landor's couplet seems to sum up the basic idea in this segment of the **Dhammapada**;

> One crowded hour of glorious life
> is worth an age without a name.

To the Buddha, what matters most is the quality and essence of life, not its span. One may live a hundred years, but only chasing shadows and illusions—a life of sound and fury signifying nothing.

So, a single insightful line in a short poem may move one more profoundly than a long epical narrative of a thousand pages. Far more difficult it is to conquer one's own self than to subjugate a thousand soldiers.

There is profound realism in the Buddha's teaching when he says that a moment's dedication to a sage is far more rewarding than performing a thousand rituals. Futile is, therefore, a long stretch of life as compared with a single day of unblemished existence.

TENS OF HUNDREDS

Weightier than a discourse of a thousand idle words is just one meaningful word that brings solace to a vexed mind. More touching to the heart is just one verse, reflective and incisive, than a thousand rambling lines in a long poem. Remember that one verse of Dharma scores over a hundred poems, comprising stanzas with sound but no meaning.

Conquering one's own self is far more glorious than vanquishing an army of a thousand soldiers. So try to win the battle over yourself instead of subduing others. Then, no force would be able to turn your triumph into defeat, your success into failure.

Remember that a moment's veneration for someone wise and saintly is far better than engaging oneself in a thousand rituals, spanning a hundred years. Far more rewarding is a moment lived wisely than keeping a ritual fire burning in a forest for countless years.

Your offerings—money, property or food—to win the gods' blessings cannot measure up to even a fraction of your veneration for the enlightened. If you revere the enlightened and follow them along the divine path, you will be blessed with four gifts—a long life-span, health, handsomeness and, above all, peace and joy.

A single day spent in wisdom and purity scores over a hundred years of life with a mind tainted, indisciplined and steeped in ignorance. Far better it is to spend a single day wisely than to waste a week purposelessly and slothfully. A single day of freedom and enlightenment eclipses a hundred years of bondage and folly.

A single day's vision of *nirvana*, of life transcending death, is far more fulfilling than a hundred years bound to the wheel of pain and suffering. A single day dedicated to Dharma is much better than a hundred years squandered away in sinful existence.

Chapter Nine

Commentary

After years of wandering through the cities and forests of India, what the Buddha saw during the night of his enlightenment under the *bodhi* tree in Gaya, was a simple vision of life. He realized that a man must be judged not by his pious resolutions or lofty speeches, but by his deeds. If the play is the thing, it is a man's action that shows his true inner being.

If an evil deed brings in its wake only pain, a virtuous action is the soul's sustenance. So let every man make it his second nature to do good unto others, and avoid any evil deed. Because there is no escape from a man's evil actions, no matter where he may try to hide himself—in a cellar, a cave, atop a hill or anywhere. An evil deed may bring one happiness for a short while, but it will be like a passing cloud, followed by a scorching sun of misery and suffering.

BLEMISHED CONDUCT

Lose no time in doing some good, and keeping yourself away from evil. If you close the door to virtue, evil will sneak in through a side window.

If you have lapsed into some evil deed, do not let it grow into a habit. Be like a wayfarer who may fall into a pit once, but who learns to walk cautiously and prudently thereafter. Out of the womb of a misdeed is born only suffering. But if you learn to engage yourself in virtuous actions, making it your second nature, you will savour eternal joy and peace.

An evil-doer who plants a seed in a field may feel happy till the harvest is ripe. But he will then eat only the bitter fruits of what he has sown—pain and suffering. On the other hand, a virtuous man may have to endure pain so long as the harvest of his noble deeds is not ripe. But then will fall into his hands the well-deserved fruits—tranquillity and happiness.

Let no man delude himself into saying: "I'll escape sorrow," while he is engaged in evil deeds. Day by day, the burden of sin will grow heavier and heavier on his shoulders, like a leaking boat into which keeps seeping water till it sinks. On the other hand, let no man take his good deeds lightly and say to himself: "Unhappiness is my lot." For day by day, the cup of his joy will keep filling up till it is brimful with peace and joy. Just as a wealthy merchant on a lone journey skirts perilous bypaths, just as someone who wishes to live happily does not touch poison, so should every man shun evil actions.

If your hand does not carry any bruises, you may even hold poison in it, fearlessly—no harm will come to you as you have not hurt anyone. But if you cause injury to a pure and innocent man, this evil will recoil upon yourself. Like the dust that is hurled against the wind only returns to the thrower's own eyes.

While the unblemished attain *nirvana* as a reward for their virtuous deeds, the evil-doers are trapped in the wheel of birth and death, doomed to eternal suffering.

Nowhere is any refuge possible for an evil-doer. No escape for him from death, anywhere—in the sky, ocean, valley or on hilltop. Yama, the god of Death, will get such a person anywhere, anytime.

Chapter Ten

Commentary

Sanctity of life is a central credo of Buddhism. There is no greater evil than killing a living creature. This is the point on which Buddhism and Christianity converge, for one of the Commandment says: "Thou shalt not kill."

Every human being dreads punishment and death. So if a man loves his own life, why should he kill any creature, or become the cause of destruction in any form?

Happiness is both for the giver and the taker. So how can a man be happy by hurting someone else? Similarly, tender speech is both for the speaker and the listener. How can one be happy by hurling abuses at somebody else?

The Buddha always reminds all men of the inevitability of death and the life hereafter. He warns every evil-doer that he will be doomed to suffer in the next life. So returns the great Master to his basic teaching—be virtuous and well-disciplined to attain eternal peace.

NEMESIS

The phantom of punishment pursues everyone. Like you, everyone is afraid of Death. So you should not kill or be the cause of death of any creature—man, bird or animal. Because every creature cherishes life, just as you do.

If you seek happiness and yet hurt those who also want to be happy, you will be cursed with misery, both here and in the life hereafter. On the other hand, if in your pursuit of happiness you also help others, you will be blessed with joy in this life and the next.

Speak tenderly to everybody and the others will also respond in words, gentle and kind. Unkind words hurled at others rebound on the foul-mouthed speaker himself. If your mind is mute like a fractured gong, you have attained the state of *nirvana*, freedom from all suffering. Just as a cowherd's staff leads the cows to pastures new and fresh, so do old age and death lead humans to new abodes of existence. Little do the selfish and cruel know what they will reap for their evil deeds after death. Bound will they be forever to the wheel of fire and burn in the flames of their own evil deeds.

If a man hurts an innocent person, pain will come to him in ten different guises—sorrow, ill-health, tragic accident, incurable disease, mental derangement, prosecution by law, public wrath, death of some dear one, loss in trade, or his house engulfed in fire. And after death, he will burn in the eternal fire of misery and pain.

If a man's heart is not without blemish, there is no salvation for him, even if he inflicts upon himself all sorts of austerities—fasting, sleeping on dust-layered ground, squatting motionlessly, keeping hair ungroomed, or doing all kinds of penance. For it's not the body but the mind that must be controlled. But one whose mind is poised and untainted, who has bridled his senses and forsaken violence, is a genuine monk. A real brahmin is he even if he is not robed in saffron.

Just as a well-trained horse does not need its rider's whip, a disciplined mind does not require anyone's prodding to be virtuous. So be like a well-groomed horse, fast and spirited, skilled to overcome suffering with faith, meditation and unflinching adherence to Dharma. That way lies *nirvana*.

Finally, just as a farmer channels water to his field, an archer trains his arrow at the bull's eye and a carpenter chisels wood into any shape he likes, so does a wise man mould his life in accordance with the norms of Dharma.

Chapter Eleven

Commentary

The Buddha first encountered old age when he rode out with Channa, his charioteer, into the heart of Kapilavastu and saw a man, pale and wrinkled, on the threshold of death. That provoked him into deep introspection. Wasn't the body a fragile mud-house, prone to decay and extinction? So why should mortals lose themselves to revelry when the end is so gruesome—the flesh and bones consigned to flames?

It is only the constant awareness of death that can keep humans away from evil-doing. Like death, old age is inevitable. Everything that blossoms, flower or youth, must wilt away—a rose sheds its petals, a fair face deepens into sunken cheeks and wrinkles on the forehead. So youth is the time when one should plant good deeds to ensure a rich harvest in old age. For anyone who has realised this, there shall be neither old age nor death.

AGE

When the world is up in flames, then why these bursts of laughter—why this wanton revelry? Engulfed in darkness, don't you want to step out of your self into light?

This body is only a painted thing, doomed to disease, decline and extinction—enlivened only by thoughts, transient like passing clouds. Let every man remember that there will be no pleasure for him when death ultimately throws away his white bones, like gourds in autumn. This body is only an unstable house, with flesh and blood inhabited by arrogance, deception, old age and death. Even a royal chariot loses its pristine glitter with the passage of time—so does the human body ultimately lose its vigour and health. What defies all these infirmities is nobility of the soul.

Like a bullock is the man
who has not learnt from his life's
journey;
who has only grown in years, but
not in wisdom.

I have traversed through endless cycles of birth and death, hoping vainly to meet the architect of my body (says the Buddha). Painfully grinding is the wheel of birth and death. But now that I have glimpsed you, O architect of my body, I shall not let you build it again. There it now lies—its beams twisted and warped and its dome demolished. My self vanquished, I am now ripe for *nirvana*.

A man, who has not undergone any spiritual discipline in his youth, is doomed to languish away in his old age, sighing and groaning over his past. He is like an old crane perched on the bank of a lake, without a fish to catch. Like a fractured bow, he lies in the autumn of his life. Like an old lion he sits idly in his den unable to hunt any more (says the Buddha).

Chapter Twelve

Commentary

Self-reliance and self-control constitute the bedrock of Buddhism. Ceaselessly should a man remember that he has to be his own monitor and his own guide. One should not use anybody else as one's crutches to move forward in life. Listen to the voice within your own self.

But before a man decides to be his own guide, he must nurture his reasoning faculty to distinguish between right and wrong.

An evil deed done harms the doer himself and affords an opportunity to his detractors to see him caught like a spider in its own web. One should never forget that while it is easy to lapse into sin, it is very difficult to follow the path of virtue.

The Buddha considers all those people foolish who debunk the virtuous and the enlightened. Their scoffing only reveals their own base self and their vulnerability to evil.

Strait is the gate to Dharma. The path is long, circuitous and hazardous, but the voyage ends in perennial bliss.

SELF

If you cherish your self dearly, protect it steadfastly, like a candle from the wind—even if you have to keep awake during one of the three segments of the night.

Teach yourself what is right, then share it with others as do the enlightened ones, who are like the sun that radiates light during the day. Or like the moon that beams its silver during the night.

Before you offer to lead others, be your own beacon light for it's more difficult to guide your own steps than to direct others.

Who else could be your ruler but your own self? Once you have disciplined it, you have a guide within your own being who will never let you down. Like the pole-star that escorts a lone wayfarer to his destination.

The evil deed of a selfish man crushes him, like a diamond that splits a tough gem. Like a vine coiling round a tree, evil strangulates its doer—and that's how his enemies would like to see him trapped. Easy it is to do some evil, but far more difficult it is to engage oneself in a good action. Just as it is easier to slide down a slope than to climb upward.

Like the *Khattaka* tree which withers away after yielding fruit, unwise people are the cause of their own downfall. Such people debunk the teachings of the enlightened, the virtuous and the holy, and adopt only the false principles of life.

When a man does evil, he causes himself injury. Shun evil, therefore, and you will be salvaged from misery and suffering. It is for each man to choose between good and evil, between rose and thorn, between light and darkness. Nobody can help another person in achieving self-realization.

Understand your duty to yourself and to others and perform it whole-heartedly. Be like an obedient charioteer who takes his master wherever he wants to go.

Chapter Thirteen

Commentary

Falsehood in any form should be avoided, says the Buddha—false principles of life and the crooked ways of the world. For the world is an illusion, transitory like a shadow that will forsake the body as soon as darkness descends.

Most humans remain enmeshed in their worldly pursuits. But those who succeed in undoing these chains escape Death and attain *nirvana*. Life after death is a reality, according to the **Dhammapada**; those who brush it aside as a fantasy are prone to evil.

Generosity liberates the soul, says the Buddha. Heaven is not for those who waste their lives in hoarding, not sharing. One should walk steadfastly on the road to Dharma, to attain bliss that eclipses all other pleasures, even lordship over the three worlds.

THIS WORLD

The way to disaster is to imitate the ways of the world—live thoughtlessly, practise devious ways and follow false doctrines.

Open your eyes and shake off sloth. Choose the straight path to virtue, avoiding any bylanes that will lead you into falsehood. You will then be blessed with endless happiness, both here and in the life beyond.

If you remember that this world is only a bubble in a pond, a mirage in the desert of life, the god of Death will not be able to demolish you. If you look closely at life, does it not look like a king's painted chariot that will soon lose its lustre? Not the foolish, but only the wise can see through the veils of life's illusions.

When an unwise man acquires knowledge, he radiates light to everyone around, like the moon shedding its silver through the clouds. When a man's virtuous actions far excel his bad deeds, he shines like the moonlight filtering through the clouds, illuminating all objects. Those who can see through the darkness of the world are like the caged birds which have flown out into freedom. What carries the swan along the sun's path is its vitality. This is the way the enlightened ones soar skyward to Heaven, vanquishing Mara and his retinue.

He who violates the fundamental norms of life, indulges in false speech or derides the life hereafter, is prone to any evil.

The abode of the gods is not for misers who are like a cobra guarding a treasure. They don't know that the way to possess is to give, for sharing alone liberates the soul. The enlightened ones on the other hand are generous—for this is the path to Heaven.

> One step towards *nirvana* is far more
> rewarding than suzerainty over the
> earth, than conquering the kingdom
> of gods, or lordship over the three
> worlds.

Chapter Fourteen

Commentary

A believer in reincarnation, the Buddha reminds man that human birth is a divine boon. But still more fortunate is he who has tamed his mind to perform only good deeds and freed himself from the taint of desire, for not even the treasures of three worlds can bring him inner peace.

To savour this peace, one need not wander about—retreat into forests or caves, or visit holy places. Peace is right there within each human being. What, then, is the way to ultimate enlightenment? The answer is simple and direct—the noble eightfold path:

Right perception
Right thought
Right speech
Right action
Right pattern of life
Right effort
Right mindfulness
Right concentration

The Buddha also exhorts man to practise meditation and be moderate in sleeping or eating. In other words, the way to happiness is the Middle Path, or the Golden Mean, as also expounded by the Greek philosophers.

THE ENLIGHTENED

An enlightened man is one whose spirit can never be vanquished and into whose spiritual territory nobody else can trespass.

How can one recognise such a man, the Buddha asks. He is not subject to any outward forces, nor can he be described in any ordinary language. This enlightened man is emancipated from every desire and every form of temptation or passion. Even the gods would envy such a man—engrossed as he always is in meditation, blessed with inner tranquillity and freedom.

Hard it is to be born a human, harder still to spend one's life like a human being, harder also to comprehend the Dharma—but the hardest of all is the road to *nirvana*.

This, in sum, is what the Buddha preaches:

Lend not yourself to evil,
nurture virtue in your body and soul,
cleanse your mind of all taint,
practise patience that endures,

oppress not your fellow humans
nor cause them any hurt,
criticise not others, for that
impoverishes the soul,
be temperate in eating and sleeping
and meditate on the loftiest.

This is the golden path to *nirvana*,
the way of the Buddhas.

Even a rain of gold coins cannot satiate one's yearning for greed and flesh. Even heavenly pleasures cannot satisfy human desires. The true devotees of the Buddha are, therefore, those who understand that passions are fickle like the seasons—that they generate only suffering and anxiety. So the way to peace is to subjugate one's passions.

The phantom of fear pursues humans everywhere. No safety is there from it even if a man escapes to mountains, forests, or holy places. How can one overcome fear when one's mind is always gripped by it, waking or dreaming?

The only safe haven is the path of virtue and the company of the wise. Comprehend the four Divine Truths: pain, its origin, its end and the Eightfold Path that will help you overcome suffering. This is the best panacea for all ills, the sole haven of peace and joy. When you understand this, pain and anxiety will fall off like the leaves of a tree in autumn, awaiting spring.

A true Buddha is rare to meet—such an enlightened one is not born in every age. But when he is born, mankind is redeemed, virtue blossoms and evil is annihilated.

The moment for rejoicing arrives
when the Buddha is born,
where the Dharma is practised,
where humans live in the Sangha,
in peace and harmony,
where the Buddha, his devotees and
the sagacious ones—in brief,
all those who have crossed the
river of suffering, are revered,
where eternal peace
reigns, and fear has no dominion.

Chapter Fifteen

Commentary

All humans are engaged in the pursuit of pleasure, but very few can fathom what it really is. True pleasure lies in liberation from hatred, fear, greed and lust—and disease, for health is a boon given to man by the gods.

It is sometimes observed that Buddhism is a religion of despair, of sorrow. But this is far from the real truth. Any man who strives to detach himself from desire, the real genesis of pain, can taste full joy—for life is to be lived happily, not sorrowfully.

The way to happiness is to live in harmony with all human beings around us, not striving to subjugate others to our will. This is a truth also articulated by Abraham Lincoln who said:

> As I would not be a slave,
> I would not be a master.

The Buddha attaches great importance to the company of friends and teachers we choose. If apparel proclaims the man, he is also judged by the company he keeps. So we should choose as our companions only the best amongst our relatives, friends and mentors, for they will add to the pleasure and zest of our life.

HAPPINESS

Let us live the life of happiness, returning hatred with forgiveness. No anger or hatred even against those who have contempt for us. Like a dog that licks the hand of its master even though it has been chidden by him.

Let us savour health and happiness, never falling sick amidst illness all around—a life free from disease, physical or mental.

Let detachment bring us happiness so that we may live unlike those who are chained by selfish bonds. It is possible to live in peace even among those who have not liberated themselves from the shackles of attachment. Be not like the mother-monkey who holds to her chest her dead baby till it falls off.

Happiness is for those who hoard not, even when everybody else around is grabbing.

> Live like birds that hold no granaries, no containers of water, just taking whatever comes their way from nature, ever enjoying peace and happiness. Be not a vanquisher, for the victorious always live in misery. Just as you wouldn't be a slave to anyone, don't lord over any man as his master. That is the way to poise and happiness.
>
> Lust is a fire that scorches both body and soul. There is no illness like anger and hatred, and there is no repose for those who remain alienated from their fellow humans. There is no sickness like avarice, and no sorrow like a self-consuming passion. If you comprehend this, you are already on your way to *nirvana*, the loftiest bliss.
>
> Health is a man's greatest boon, and contentment is his most precious treasure. If you repose faith in your close relatives, and drink the sacred wine of Dharma in your deepest thoughts, you'll be emancipated from anxiety and evil.

Fortunate is the man who meets the enlightened ones, and luckier is the man who can spend his life in their company. If you cherish happiness, shun the company of the unwise.

Like the moon's glow amidst the fraternity of the stars, living with the sagacious brings one happiness —it is like returning to one's family after a long absence. On the other hand, living with the unwise is like walking a long way with an enemy who may harm you anytime. It is like keeping a wild animal as your pet.

So seek the company of the enlightened who are virtuous, tolerant, compassionate and understanding.

Chapter Sixteen

Commentary

This section looks at joy from some related angles. Meditation, the recurring theme in the **Dhammapada,** is one of the divinest pathways to inner happiness. Through introspection one may learn to distinguish between pleasure that is perennial and that which is ephemeral. The latter generates only suffering.

If a man seeks pleasure in worldly pursuits, selfish and trivial, he is sliding downhill, not climbing up to real bliss. But the way uphill is arduous, strewn with briars and brambles. So it can be traversed only with sterling will and indefatigable stamina.

Virtuous actions are a man's best companions on his voyage to real pleasure, both in this world and the life hereafter.

JOY

Don't seek the wordly pleasures of life, forgetting
that meditation alone will bring you
real joy. A man who is oblivious of
his real aim in life, and remains
deeply embroiled in sensual pleasures,
will some day realize the primacy of
meditation as the only true source
of bliss.

Not being able to enjoy a pleasure generates pain;
encountering anything unpleasant
also brings anguish. Then why not
transcend both pain and pleasure
to achieve inner peace?

Attachment to any person or object will only
cause distress. But when one has gone
beyond all opposites—light and shade,
pain and pleasure, rose and cactus—
one has attained true freedom.

Fear and pain are the offspring of attachment;
so release yourself from anxiety and
suffering. But this is possible only if
you are rid of worldly bonds.

Grief and fear are born of selfish entanglements.
If you have emancipated yourself from
all such bonds, you will be rid of fear and
pain. You'll then be free like a bird in the
air, or like a fish in the sea.

Frustration, despondency and fear are
born of selfish pleasures. If you
free yourself from the taint of
selfishness, you will be released
from both dread and disillusionment.

Chapter Seventeen

Commentary

In the hierarchy of human failings, anger stands next to lust, according to the sastras. But in a spurt of uncontrollable rage, it may consume all other passions. The conquest of anger then becomes man's hardest battle to win.

In a poem titled "Anger", I have tried to visualise this emotion in its stark form.

> If it was only a feeble tremor
> on the Richter scale,
> then why did the sun feel unhinged
> and disgorge all its fireballs
> on the earth?
> His own eyes were the prime witness
> to the holocaust—
> their bloodshot veins throbbed
> on the radar screen, signalling doom
> to an epoch of warm intimacy.
> Tempered in the oven of a sizzling
> throat, even human teeth may grow
> into tusks, charging at giant windmills.

(From **Thus Spake the Buddha**)

What, then, is the way to vanquish anger, when the eyes glow like red embers, the body loses its balance and the tongue spits venom? The Buddha's answer is—kindness, forgiveness, compassion and understanding. That was also what Mahatma

Gandhi had learnt from the Bible. If someone slaps you on one cheek, present him the other. This will demolish him more effectively than returning a blow with blow. The tongue should be used not as a weapon to hurt someone, but only as a healing balm.

ANGER

Renounce anger, also pride. And rid yourself of all worldly entanglements—family, property and fame. Free are all those humans from sorrow who never care to possess other people and objects, or try to claim them as their own. That way lies bondage and misery.

If you can muzzle your anger, as you hold back a chariot that is about to roll out of control, you are a skilled charioteer. The unskilled one will hold the reins idly in his hands.

Kindness alone can vanquish wrath, like a sprinkle of water subduing a flame. Let gentleness conquer unkindness, magnanimity overcome avarice and the light of truth dispel the darkness of falsehood. Never lapse into untruth, nor lose temper. Keep your hands open to give even if you don't have much to spare. This is the way to win divine blessing.

So, engage yourself only in worthy actions which will bring you peace, not pain. Fortify yourself both inwardly and outwardly, like a fortress raised with high ramparts and massive gates. Don't waste any time, because every moment squandered away carries you downwards.

The way down is for those

who are ashamed of an action they
should not regret and

who are not regretful of an action
they should be ashamed of.

Such men uphold wrong principles of life. Also, destined to slide downward are those

who are afraid of what they need
not fear—and those

who are not afraid of what they need
to fear.

Also will go downward those
who perceive untruth where it doesn't exist and
who don't perceive untruth where it does exist.

But a man who has seen the light of truth will climb his way upward, progressively.

Chapter Eighteen

Commentary

Not so much the cleanliness of the body, as the purity of the mind, because that alone will prepare a man for his last journey to the other world. Death, in the Buddha's teaching, is the point from which a man may look back to evaluate his life's actions, good or bad. Most humans are, therefore, not adequately prepared to face Yama, the god of Death.

What kind of preparation does a man need to encounter his last moments with serene composure? The piety of his soul and his adherence to the tenets of the Dharma. To cleanse one's mind one must overcome jealousy, the green-eyed monster, remain chaste like a virgin, abstain from killing any creature, renounce anger and arrogance, not desire another man's wife and forgive others for their weaknesses.

If a man is armed with these virtues, he is ready to unfurl the sails of his soul's boat to cross the river of life to the other shore where there will be no more sorrow and no more birth and death.

IMPIETY

Like a wilted flower is man, waiting for Yama, the god of Death. Remember, you'd soon have to set out on a long voyage, but are you ready for it? There's the boat to ferry you across the river of life to the dark shore of death. But are you holding the oars tightly in hand and are the boat's sails prim and unfurled?

Let the light of wisdom glow in your soul and don't let its flame ever flicker or go out. Purity and innocence are like the wick and oil in an earthen lamp that will keep you forever away from darkness.

Are you aware that you are on the last leg of your voyage, that Yama is knocking at your door? There shall be no respite for you during this voyage, only travail and suffering. And you are still not ready for it! Like a listless traveller, you wander through a dark forest, unaided.

Let the torch of wisdom remain aglow in your soul, forever. Let purity and innocence be your protector—to salvage you from the grinding wheel of birth and death.

Let your mind glisten like the gold after the goldsmith has blown off all the impurities from it. Just as rust nibbles at an iron bar which breeds it, so do tainted actions consume all those who are engaged in them.

A chant grows feeble if not repeated, like the refrain in a song. A dwelling falls apart if not repaired in time and the body begins to sag if not regularly exercised. So will a night watchman doze off if he does not remain up on his feet.

Immodesty is a great failing in a woman. A hand niggardly in giving is blemished. Actions steeped in selfishness lack merit, both in this life and the life hereafter. But the worst of all is a mind that is lost in the dark cave of ignorance. Light the torch of wisdom and you will shine like the moon in a dark night.

Easy is life for a man who has forsaken all sense of shame. No better than a crow is he who is a manipulator of mischief and is arrogant and immoral. But difficult is the voyage of life for one who practises humility, kindness and detachment—whose life is untainted like a lotus.

They will lie in the graves, dug by their own hands

who indulge in killing any creature

who take to lying like a dishonest
trader

who ache to grab somebody else's
wealth

who lust for another man's wife
and

who let wine turn their heads.

Since the human mind is a soft prey to evil, don't let avarice and vice lead you to a life of sorrow and suffering—because a poorly thatched hut is always leaking.

Some men there are who make offerings out of faith, while others do it out of warm friendship. But you need not feel jealous of those who receive such gifts, for if you do so this will keep you in a perpetual state of mental turmoil. On the other hand, those who are free from the taint of jealousy bask in the eternal sunshine of tranquillity.

Remember that there is
no flame like carnal desire
no jailer like hatred
no trap like wanton passion and
no flood like avarice.

Easy it is for anyone to pick holes in others' actions and filter them drop by drop. But far more difficult it is to scrutinise one's own failings. Everyone tries to conceal them, like a gambler hiding a losing move.

But if a man keeps harping on the infirmities of others, his own frailties grow more and more grievous, till they become almost uncontrollable like a boulder rolling down a slope, gathering momentum every moment.

Just as there is no charted path in the limitless sky, there is no haven for those who are slaves to their desires. But the Buddha's votaries live emancipated from all worldly embroilments. You should always remember that life is caught up in a ceaseless flux, like children swinging up and down a magic wheel. But the believers in the Buddha transcend this flux, remaining eternally stable in a state of being. They are like the pole-star that remains constant amidst a multitude of other stars.

Chapter Nineteen

Commentary

The Buddha is essentially an apostle of non-violence, peace and compassion. In a world torn apart by wars and terror, his gospel of non-violence seems to be the only panacea for our ills.

To the Buddha, verbalisation in any form is a travesty of truth. Not by talking, discoursing or analysing can a man experience the divine truth—but only by right action.

Nor do a man's outward trappings hold any mirror to his inner self. Neither his grey hair nor his professed silence, nor his shaven head can make him an enlightened person. To attain true wisdom, one must transcend all opposites—good and bad, happiness and suffering. This concept of transcendence emerges as a basic theme in most Indian scriptures—the **Gita**, the **Upanishads, the Guru Granth Sahib**—and in the teachings of Lord Mahavir, the founder of Jainism.

PRACTISING DHARMA

Those who use violent means to achieve their goal in life have gone far away from the Dharma. But those who, knowing right from wrong, truth from falsehood, lead others through non-violence to Truth, are genuine votaries of the Dharma. They are truly enlightened, Buddhas.

He who talk too much is alienated from wisdom—for then even a parrot could claim to articulate words of divinity. Only he is truly sagacious

who believes in good deeds, not just
idle words,

who is patient and enduring like a
tiller, ploughing his field in
rain or sunshine,

who is emancipated from fear and
hatred, and is always at peace with
himself. He is like a tortoise
that has withdrawn its organs
under its cover.

Dharma is not for those who discourse about it, preaching it in the market-place. But it is for those who have learnt to live virtuously, in love with all fellow human beings—even if they are not well-versed in the scriptures. For the way to *nirvana* is through deeds, not words.

Grey hair is no sign of age or wisdom, for every old man may not be fully baked in the oven of life. On the other hand, a truly aged man is he

who is truthful like an unsullied
mirror,

who is noble like a sage,
who is meek and gentle like a
new-shorn lamb,

who has reined in his desires like a
horse well-groomed, and

whose mind is untainted like lustral
water.

Beauty resides not

in words spoken genially—

in a face, fair and attractive, nor

in a person consumed with jealousy
and selfishness.

True beauty shines only in a person who
has rid his mind of all taints.

A shaven head does not make a monk, nor does his saffron robe. A true Buddha is he

who is master of his self, like a
skilled horse-rider,

who always speaks the truth and

who has banished all base desires.

A genuine monk is he who has burnt all his passions to ashes, and has risen like a new being.

Going with a begging bowl from door to door, does not make a true *Bhikshu*. He can claim to be one only

if he lives in harmony with Dharma,

if he is pure like fresh milk, or a lump
of unadulterated gold,

if he has transcended all opposites
good and evil
heat and cold
light and shade
joy and sorrow,

if he walks through life's market-place but
not attracted by any object—
for detachment is the key that
opens the golden portals to
nirvana.

Keeping one's lips sealed in silence does not make one enlightened, if one is still seeped in ignorance. He alone is sagacious who holds the scales of discernment steadily in both hands, choosing truth and discarding falsehood—like the winnower who blows off the chaff from the wheat.

Nobility lies in not hurting any living creature, for all life is sacred—man, beast or flower. So don't injure anyone.

The way to *nirvana*, to eternal peace
and joy, is not through rituals,
alms-giving, nor through pious
resolutions, nor through study
of scriptures, nor chanting of
mantras, nor through celibacy,

nor even through meditation—
eyes shut, sitting cross-legged.

Only by subjugating one's ego can one savour the golden fruit of eternal bliss.

Chapter Twenty

Commentary

Distrustful of the obscurantist sophistry of some sastras, the Buddha chose to speak to the common man in a language that was simple and transparent. In the moment of his enlightenment under the *bodhi* tree at Gaya, what he realized was a simple and practical way of liberation from sorrow. As a pragmatic sage, he just pointed to the Eightfold Path for any man, of high or low caste, to attain *nirvana*. No chanting of mantras, no abstruse exegesis of the concept of Brahma or the Oversoul.

Of equal simplicity and direction, as his Eightfold Path, is his gospel of the four Noble Truths. He observes that

> human life is synonymous with
> pain (*dukha*),
> disillusionment,
> misery and
> tension.
>
> These are generated by a man's
> ego and desire (*tantra*).
>
> But liberation from all suffering is
> possible for man through
> the Eightfold Path which is
> the golden avenue to *nirvana*.

It may be seen that this teaching constitutes a perfect synthesis of practice and precept—showing all mankind the path to *Dharma* (truthfulness).

THE PATHWAY TO DHARMA

Of all the paths to *nirvana*, the Eightfold Path stands out supreme; of all the truths, the Noble Four Truths are the best; of all the states of mind, detachment is the most rewarding; and of all human beings, the enlightened ones are the most blessed.

This Dharma is the only bleach for cleansing the mind—like bleaching a soiled cloth of all dirt. If you adopt this Dharma you will vanquish Mara, the Tempter. This will release you from all pain and sorrow. This is the truth I have proclaimed (says the Buddha), after the shafts of suffering fell away from me, blunted and bent.

But all this has to be done by self-endeavour, for the Buddha can only point toward the path. All effort has to be one's own only. Like a fledgling sparrow that must learn to fly on its own wings. Like a tigress' cub that must learn to hunt on its own. So if we follow the Eightfold Path and practise meditation, Mara will lose his dominion over us.

What most humans don't realize is that life is transient, a mere shadow that will vanish at dusk, a passing cloud that will melt into the sky. This realization alone will salvage a man from sorrow and pain and help him attain ultimate wisdom.

If we remember that sorrow is our innate inheritance, that we are born in our mother's pain and die in our own, then we will be released from misery and suffering and the light of wisdom will shine on our forehead.

Wisdom will descend upon us like divine light if we comprehend that true divinity is liberation from self. If we hold this truth in our mind, no sorrow will come our way.

It is only when one is in the bloom of youth and health that one should wake up to self-realization. He who is enmeshed in the web of indecision, who fumbles and falters, will never reach the peak of ultimate wisdom. Let us keep under constant surveillance all our thoughts, words and actions.

If wisdom is born out of meditation, ignorance is the child of an unreflective mind. Let us watch our steps, ever mindful of what will carry us forward into light and what will hold us back in darkness.

The way to freedom is to axe all the trees in our forest of desires, not just one tree. Then alone shall we stand on the open ground of eternal release from all bondage—of self and sorrow.

If even a vestige of carnal desire lingers in our mind, like a calf clinging to its mother's udders, we will remain sunk in the morass of misery. So let us pull out every desire by its roots, just as we would nip off a lotus during autumn. We should adopt a mentor who is familiar with the road to *nirvana* and then follow him unswervingly.

> This will be my winter retreat.
>
> That house will be my abode during
> the monsoons,
>
> and I'll move to this residence
> during the summer.

Lost in these fantasies, a man will become oblivious of the ultimate end—Death. For Yama, the god of Death, may strike when a man is wrapped in his dreams—his family and worldly belongings. The monsoon downpour will then sweep him off his feet just as an insurgent flood will inundate and wipe away a village immersed in deep slumber.

When the black raven of Death descends upon us with its ominous wings, nobody will shield us from it—our parents or our children. So let us not waver or falter on the pathway to Dharma which alone will lead us to *nirvana*.

Chapter Twenty One

Commentary

In this section of the **Dhammapada**, the Buddha dwells on a variety of themes, central to attaining freedom from sorrow.

True votaries of the Buddha are always immersed in thoughts about the Dharma. Eternally vigilant, they are conscious of the need to abjure all sensory pleasures, to live a life of solitude and introspection.

Human existence is a twofold trap—painful it is to live in this world and equally agonising to leave it. The only way out of this labyrinth is to vanquish desire, particularly lust which is the arch enemy of man. No wonder, *Kama*, craving for flesh, blindfolds man and leads him to abysmal sin.

VERSES OF DIVERSE HUES

If a man experiences a higher pleasure and thereafter a lesser one, will he not return to the former? Like someone who, having tasted a sweet fruit, will not opt for anything less delicious.

A man who pitches his happiness on the misery of others will find himself caught in a web of hatred, like a fish trapped in a fisherman's net.

Do not hesitate to engage yourself in doing something that is worthy to be done, and do not lend yourself to an action that should be avoided. Or else, the weight of suffering on you will grow heavier and heavier. Only through meditation and self-control will you be able to distinguish between a worthy action and that which is unworthy. Such a realization will steer you through sorrow to peace and happiness.

There are three things that must be exterminated—ego, lust, and wanton passions. These are the arch enemies of man. A true Brahmin is one who has subjugated them all, specially the self-will that blindfolds a man on his journey to self-realization.

All true followers of the Buddha are always
fully conscious and vigilant, like an
alert watchman—their thoughts
are ever riveted on their mentor,
waking or dreaming,

deeply immersed in the Dharma,
day and night—their minds
converging on the *Sangha,*
the congregator of monks, and always

intensely engaged in reining in their
senses, day and night,
ever ready to offer compassion
to any living creature.

Difficult it is to confront the last moments, and equally difficult it is to live in this world. And equally burdensome it is to be a wanderer. So focus your mind on the ultimate destination—Dharma and you will be released from all restlessness and suffering.

A man who is virtuous in deed and thought is esteemed by everyone, everywhere. Like the Himalayan peak, he shines above the terrain of ordinary men. He is visible even from a remote distance—while the common man passes by unnoticed, like an arrow shot in the dark.

If you are all by yourself—sitting, sleeping or walking about—subjugate your ego, your lower self. Eternal happiness will be yours when you have overcome all your desires. You will then be like a trainer who has broken in a wild animal to make it perform at his bidding.

Chapter Twenty Two

Commentary

If desire is the source of pain, lust is its ugly face and adultery the most heinous sin. In an age that condones sexual promiscuity as a venial human failing, the Buddha's portrayal of adultery as the culmination of guilt, fear and insecurity, should sound significantly relevant today. He describes an adulterous couple as a pair of hunted rabbits, trying in vain to escape the hunter. But how long can they dodge the public eye?

I have tried to portray the same situation in my poem "Thou shalt not commit..."—which is one of the ten Commandments:

Unhoused, we drift across the continents,
our selves in polythene bags
sealed against reproach.

We rest on treetops,
eat the dust off sidewalks, and
slither into ratholes.

We feed exotic fish in aquariums
on cankerworms of angst, wearing
tinted lenses to dodge the sun.

But darkness breathes its own nemesis.

Last night, at a wayside rest house,
as you loomed over me, like a lifeguard
resuscitating a novice diver,
and bared your deep red wound
for me to kiss, I heard, in the caverns
of silence, my son's mother break into
a hyena's snigger:
'How's it going? Happy?'

THE WAY DOWN

A man who speaks what is false and the other who disowns his past, are both doomed to the way down. Both of them are accomplices in falsehood—here and after death.

He who dons the saffron robe but has not given up ill-manners and indiscipline, slides down to the dark pit. Far better it is for such a monk to swallow a blazing hot rod of iron than to sustain himself on doles of charity from his devotees.

A man who commits adultery loses esteem, invites blame from everyone and is doomed to more and more pain. What joy can there be for such a person who feels scared, lying in the arms of another, equally scared. Both are on the run like hunted animals, living in a perpetual fear of nemesis.

A man can cut his finger if he handles a blade of *Kusha* grass, carelessly. So can asceticism, practised unwisely, send a man sliding downward.

A pledge not honoured, an ideal of chastity not scrupulously followed, a deed not performed dutifully—all these earn one no recompense. If there is anything worthy to be done, do it whole-heartedly. An ascetic who is not fully initiated will find himself covered with a heavier and heavier layer of dust.

Remember that all evil deeds engender pain. So lend yourself only to virtuous actions which will bring you solace. Protect yourself properly, both inwardly and outwardly. Be like a fortress with lofty ramparts and impregnable iron gates. Don't squander away a single moment, for time is always on the wings of an invisible bird. Opportunities wasted in life will push you downward.

If you are regretful of an action for which you need not repent, or if you are not regretful for something that you should have not done, in both cases you are sliding downward, because you are following wrong principles of life.

If you are apprehensive where you need not be, and are not afraid when there is need for fear, then also you have forsaken the true principles of life. That is the way downward.

If a man sees error where it is not there, and does not see it where it exists, he too is sliding downward because he has strayed away from the path of righteousness.

But if a man perceives life in right perspective—sees error where it exists and sees no fault where it does not exist, he is progressing upward because he is following the correct norms of life. He is like someone who looks into a mirror that does not distort images.

Chapter Twenty Three

Commentary

Since the Buddha is essentially a poet, he thinks and feels in terms of metaphors and images. He uses animals, birds and natural objects as his symbols—horses, chariots, cart-drivers, swans, rivers and so on.

In this segment, he uses the elephant as a multifaceted metaphor—as a well-trained animal it is capable of enduring sharp arrows on a battlefield; it serves as a faithful companion to its king; as a loner in a forest it roams about at its will; and as a male in heat, it would not eat if separated from its female partner.

But what is of utmost importance is the discipline that a man or an animal must observe in order to be of any use to himself and to others. Similarly, an untrained animal—horse, mule or elephant—is like an indisciplined human mind at the mercy of vagrant thoughts and desires.

THE ELEPHANT

Let every human being learn to endure unkind words spoken by others—like the elephant that endures the wounds of arrows in the course of a battle. How very thoughtless are those who hurl barbs of unkind words at others.

Let not an untrained elephant take part in a battle—as only a well-groomed elephant can carry a king securely through a battlefield. Let a man, therefore, discipline his mind to endure the shafts of unkind words.

Mules are worthy animals when properly broken into service. But worthier are well-groomed horses and still worthier are fully trained elephants. But the loftiest among men is he who has subjugated his mind to his will. Remember that no one, howsoever disciplined, can carry you to *nirvana.* To lead you to this unknown land, only your own disciplined mind will be your torch-bearer.

When the Dhanapalaka elephant is in heat, he will not eat while bound in chains. He aches for his made in the jungle, trumpeting out his yearning.

Eat not too much, nor oversleep like a dog over-fed. It is the slothful who are doomed to the ever-grinding wheel of birth and death.

Time was (says the Buddha) when my mind wandered listlessly, desiring to do whatever it wanted. Now I am in full control of it, like the mahout who bends his elephant to his will, with his spiked staff.

Be ever-alert, fortifying your mind against all negative emotions and thoughts. Like an elephant who pulls himself out of a deep mass of mud, so should a man salvage himself from all evil ways.

If you are fortunate enough to have a friend who is wise, virtuous and warm-hearted, hold him as your companion through the voyage of life. He will help you withstand all the perils during your journey.

But if you cannot find such a friend, learn to walk alone, unaided.

Like an elephant who roams about the
forest alone at his own will, or

like a king who renounces his
kingdom to rule the territory
within his own mind.

Far better it is to live a solitary life than live with those who have not fully matured. Learn to be at peace with yourself, like an elephant who roams about alone in the forest. Lend not yourself to evil ways.

True friendship is a mutual relationship where both friends operate on the same emotional plane. But far better friends are a man's own good actions which will ferry him across the river of life to the other shore. Death will hold no terror for him as he will then transcend all sorrow and pain.

Fortunate it is to be a mother or father. Better it is to live the life of Dharma. But the best of all is to become a sage, an enlightened person.

Everlasting bliss will be yours if you are virtuous—if you nourish faith in your heart and wisdom in your mind. A man untainted in mind and heart is a blessed creature.

Chapter Twenty Four

Commentary

The central tenet of Buddhism is the conquest of desires which are man's worst enemies. They grow like cancer cells; if you control them at one point, they appear in another, till the entire body is infected.

All cravings ambush a man in various guises—as a seductive face, a pot of gold, or a public applause to one's fame. So if a man could rid himself of such longings, he would be the envy even of gods.

In a poem titled "Thus Spake the Buddha," I visualise desire as an unbridled horse:

> Desire—an unbridled stallion,
> mane incensed like Medusa's hair,
> hooves sparking on a cobbled crossroad,
> signalling restraint.
>
> Body's appetite, like a crocodile's belly,
> can hold rock, metal
> and a virgin's thigh.
>
> Under the Bodhi tree, I vanquished
> my hunger
> to bare ribs, and cheeks dented like
> little whirlpools—
> till the intestines cried out:
> "Enough!"
>
> The way to satiate a yearning
> is to sublimate it. Like lava licking
> barren earth into tulips and marigolds.

IRREPRESSIBLE URGES

The irrepressible impulses of the unwise grow like a creeper. Like a monkey, they leap from one tree to another, searching for fruits.

When these impulses incite us, suffering grows like weeds in a lawn. So if you vanquish these wanton urges, they will drop off like beads of water from a lotus leaf. If a man does not pull out such yearnings as one would the roots of *birana* grass, he will be demolished by Mara—like a strong stream sweeping away everything on its bank. Unless a man puts out the flames of his wild desires, they will waylay him, more and more compulsively—like a tree sprouting forth again if its roots are not dug out completely.

If a man allows all the streams of his desires to gush out of his mind, they will inundate him and wash him away. Such streams flow everywhere—like highwaymen out to ambush unwary travellers. Creepers of wanton passion they are, spawning everywhere. Whenever you feel such a creeper sprouting in your mind, fork it out by its root before it is too late.

All men are embroiled in attachments and yearnings for pleasure. Thirsting for these, they are enmeshed in the cobweb of birth and death. Impelled by their desires, men scamper about like hunted rabbits, sinking into greater and greater misery and pain. So there is no peace for them unless they liberate themselves from the clutches of their desires. If some men succeed in escaping from one jungle of their passions, they fall into another. So they are never entirely free from this bondage.

The enlightened ones have observed that a man may disentangle himself from the shackles of a rope or an iron chain, but it is much more difficult to free himself from the chains of family, wealth and other worldly entanglements. So snap such bonds by vanquishing all wanton desires, never returning to the illusions of sensory pleasures.

Most human beings are ensnared by their wild impulses, like a spider captured in its own web. So if you liberate yourself from this web, you will be rid of all sorrow and pain.

Supreme bliss is awaiting you there on the other bank of this river of life—but only if you renounce all that is here on this bank—everything in front, in the middle and behind you.

If you wish to cross over to the other shore, where eternal bliss awaits you, don't allow any misgiving, passion or desire to tighten your shackles. Go deep into introspection, like a saint in a cave immersed in his thoughts. Distinguish between the transient and the eternal and between a passing cloud and the day-long sunshine. This is the way to free yourself from the snare of Mara, the Tempter.

A man who has liberated himself from hunger, sin and fear has pulled out all thorns from his life. His life then is like a rose without thorns, or a fruit without worms. He will endure the burden of his body for the last time for he would have attained *nirvana*.

A man
who is in full control of himself,
who wears the garb of purity,
who has renounced all earthly ties
and
who lives a life of freedom
needs no mentor, for he has acted as his own
guide and pathfinder.

There is
no boon more satisfying than Dharma and
no boon yielding greater happiness.

Dharma alone can help one vanquish all
yearning, and release one from pain and misery.

Craze for money always haunts the greedy
but those who are in quest of
nirvana are free from this passion.

Devoid of understanding, the avaricious
inflict injury upon themselves
and those who come in contact
with them. Like foul odor, they
vitiate the atmosphere all around.

Like weeds destroying a luscious field,
avarice impairs the soul.
Therefore, venerable are those who
have rid themselves of greed.

Like weeds destroying a luscious field,
carnal desire impoverishes the soul.
So all honour to those who have
freed themselves from lust.

Like weeds destroying a luscious field,
contempt for fellow humans
debilitates the soul. So respect all
those who have conquered contempt
and hatred.

Like weeds destroying a luscious field,
selfish yearnings weaken the soul.
So respect all those who have
transcended their selfish cravings.

Chapter Twenty Five

Commentary

What is unique about the Buddha is the clarity of his perception, his capability to distinguish between illusion and reality, between a mere resolution and its actual implementation.

According to him, a Bhikshu should be judged in terms of his deeds, not dress or words. A genuine Bhikshu accomplishes the well-nigh impossible task of disciplining his mind—his ears, eyes and tongue. Contentment, self-reliance, freedom from jealousy, greed and ostentation are his distinctive traits. Like a tortoise, he has withdrawn his organs under his cover and is now indifferent to praise or censure.

Meditation is his mode of dwelling on the eternal doctrines of Dharma.

In brief, all the elements are so mixed in such a Bhikshu that even the sages might stand up and say "Here is a true manifestation of the divine soul!"

The Buddha highlights the same virtues in a Brahmin as in a Bhikshu. Just as it is not a saffron robe that makes a Bhikshu, so it is not matted hair that reveals a true Brahmin. Anyone can attain to Brahminhood by overcoming greed, lust, self-will, fear and hatred. In brief, a Brahmin is not how he looks, but what he does.

THE TRUE BHIKSHU

A genuine Bhikshu is one who has disciplined his eyes, ears and all other organs. Our senses are worthy companions only when they are controlled. Uncontrolled, they grow into wild beasts. So discipline your body into engaging itself in righteous actions only—and your tongue in noble speech. This will liberate you from the bondage of sorrow.

A true Bhikshu is one who has trained his tongue, feet and hands to serve his fellow human beings. He is always immersed in meditation to savour inward peace and permanent joy. The divine mantra is always on his lips; he is dedicated to simple living and to propagating Dharma in tender and lucid words.

Dharma is the essence of his life. On it he reflects ceaselessly, seeks his joy in it and never lets go his hold on it. For he knows that Dharma alone will release him from sorrow.

A genuine Bhikshu is one who never pines for what he has not received, nor is he consumed with jealousy for what others possess. No peace in meditation is possible for those who burn in the flames of jealousy.

Such a Bhikshu is the envy of even the gods, for he lives the life of truth and selfless dedication to the welfare of others. Liberated from any craving to possess objects and people, he does not regret over what has not come his way. With love for all humans and an unflinching faith in the Buddha's doctrines, he attains the state of peace that surpasseth all understanding.

O devout Bhikshus, let your boat be unburdened of fear and desire so that it may sail faster toward the other shore. The pathway to *nirvana* is to liberate oneself from hatred and avarice.

The way to eternal bliss is to cross the five hurdles, the five sensory attachments—taste, smell, touch, sight and sound.

Go deep into meditation, O Bhikshus, and indulge not in sensory pleasures. If you hold a red hot iron rod in your mouth, what use will it be to cry out: "I am trapped in agony!"

Meditation is not for the unenlightened, nor is wisdom for those who do not introspect. The shorter pathway to *nirvana* is to acquire wisdom through meditation, for then alone will you grow spiritually.

A Bhikshu with a disciplined mind enters any house, with his heart brimful with the divine bliss of the Dharma. If he comprehends the growth and decline of the elements that sustain the body, he will win the boon of immortality from the gods.

O Bhikshu,
strive to be sagacious
subjugate your senses like the tortoise
that withdraws at will its organs
under its shell,
remain satisfied with whatever you have,
keep company only of the unblemished
and righteous friends,
be friendly to everyone and carry
out your duties faithfully.

Then will you drink the cup of divine nectar, attain permanent peace and be released from all suffering.

A genuine Bhikshu is he who shakes off all avarice and hatred from his mind, like the *varsika* plant that drops all its withered flowers. Composed and poised is he in speech, action and thought. He has unshackled himself of all worldly bonds.

A true Bhikshu is one who strives to elevate himself by his own endeavour and acts as his own monitor and critic. For it is only through self-reliance and ceaseless vigilance that a man can reach the peak where resides eternal joy. So be your own guardian and controller and discipline your mind just as a skilled rider reins in his horse.

A genuine Bhikshu always tastes happiness and peace because he is a devotee of Dharma and is, therefore, well-equipped to cross over to the other shore, beyond the vicissitudes of life. Resplendent with the divine light, a true Bhikshu always travels along the path of Dharma, illuminating the world like moonlight in a sky without clouds.

Chapter Twenty Six

Commentary

Unlike Hinduism which recognises four orders of society, as four castes (Brahmin, Kshatriya, Vaishya and Sudra), the Buddha recognises a man's status only in terms of his actions—not birth. According to him, even a low-caste man can attain the status of Brahmin if he practises the Dharma by liberating himself from all sensory entanglements.

This has made the Buddha an apostle of universal equality and brotherhood. Also the fact that he chose Pali, the average man's language and not the elitist Sanskrit, enabled his message to reach the common man—the tiller, the trader or the cart-driver. The language used in the **Dhammapada**, almost Biblical in its simplicity and directness, touches the chords of every human heart.

A TRUE BRAHMIN

Cheerfully and courageously, sail across the river of life, subduing all your desires. Anyone who transcends the life of fragments, will comprehend the totality and eternality of the life beyond death. So if you ferry yourself across the river of attachments, likes and dislikes, you will be liberated from all shackles.

Who, then, is a genuine Brahmin? He who has transcended all passions and has gone beyond all opposites—light and dark, spring and autumn. Emancipated he is from the bond of fear.

A true Brahmin has disciplined his mind to remain poised in all circumstances in order to reach the ultimate destination of his life.

The sunlight lasts only during the day and the moonlight only during the night. The warrior's glory is only for the battle's hour, but the Brahmin's light stays as long as he is immersed in meditation. Like the Buddha, he radiates his light of love, each hour of the day and night.

Only he can claim to be a Brahmin who has shaken off every form of evil. Only he can claim to be a recluse

whose mind is composed,

whose heart is chaste like a lotus,

who never lapses into anger,

who never hurts others even if he
has been harmed by them,

who does not cause pain to others—
so no sorrow comes to him.

He alone is a true Brahmin

who does not injure others by an
unkind thought, word or
deed—for he has vanquished
his mind and body, like a
cart-driver in full control of
his bullocks,

who follows in the footsteps of the
Buddha, and

who lights his lamp with the flame of
his sacrifice and dedication.

Not by birth, nor by sporting matted hair,
can one claim to be a Brahmin, but
only by dedication to love and truth.

Futile it is to sport matted hair, and sit on
a deer skin for meditation, if one's
mind still clings to carnal desire.

A saffron apparel and outward trappings do
not make a Brahmin—only the
discipline of mind and control of

sensory attachments through ceaseless
meditation.

Not by high caste or wealth can one claim to
be a Brahmin. Anyone who succeeds
in liberating himself from all worldly
entanglements can become a Brahmin.

A true Brahmin is one
who has shaken off his fetters,
who quakes not in fear,
who has not fallen into the snare
of his personal embroilments,
who lets not any evil thought taint
his mind,
who has snapped all bonds with
karma,

who has risen from a long spell
of sleep into a new state of
awakening—to realize the
birth of a new self,

who is not afraid of imprisonment
or death,

who is endowed with the strength
of love that not even an army
can vanquish,

who has conquered anger and has
never strayed into the bypaths
of evil,

who is untainted and self-disciplined,

whose body will never again suffer
the pain of birth and death,

who yearns not for pleasure any
more than the water aching
to wet a lotus flower—any
more than a mustard seed
trying to cling to the head
of a needle. Such a man will

be emancipated from all pain.
No more burden will there
be on his shoulders.

He alone is a true Brahmin
whose sagacity is deep,
whose understanding of life is profound,
who has never gone away from
the righteous path, and has
thus climbed up to the highest
peak of bliss.

He alone is a true Brahmin
whose requirements in life are
limited,
who lives a life of detachment, keeping
himself equidistant from everyone
—householders or wandering
sadhus,
who has renounced all instruments
of war,
who has eschewed violence towards
all living creatures—humans,
animals or birds,
who abstains from killing any form
of life, nor assists anyone in
demolishing it,
who never responds to hostility
with animosity,
who remains aloof from all selfish
people,
who never forsakes peace, even
amidst war,
who has liberated himself from the
taints of pride, deception or
hatred—which have all

dropped from him like a
mustard seed from the tip of
a needle,
who is always truthful and gracious,
who is a giver, not a taker; and who
always rejoices in serving others,

who has realized that heaven is for
those who have subjugated their
desires, and liberated themselves
from every kind of blemish,

who has transcended death and the
flux of time by neither desiring
anything, nor entertaining any
misgiving about others,

who is the lord over his mind and
body, like an absolute ruler
of his kingdom,

who is not disturbed by contraries—
evil or good, night or day,

who has attained freedom from
suffering, desire and blemish,

who has transcended the duality
of life, and has rid himself
of evil or pain—who is
always luminous like the moon
in a cloudless sky,

who has sailed across a river,
turbulent and hazardous, to
safety on the other shore,

who has renounced his self,

who feels himself at home even
when he is homeless,

whose heart is brimful even when
he has emptied his mind of
his ego,

who has overcome his self-will,
forever,

who has been released from sorrow,
perennially,

who has relinquished his craving
to possess, even divine things,

who has liberated himself from
attachment to nature or fellow
human beings, and has thus
emerged as the supreme
vanquisher of the world,

who has a firm hand on the pulse
of life, its ebb and flow,

who is never conscious of his
identity, having overcome
all thoughts of *I* and *Mine*,

who will ever remain awake, never
lapsing into sleep,

whose ways of life may look
mysterious and unknowable
to the onlookers,

who has not been conquered by
time—present, past or
future—for his life is no
longer subjected to decline
and death,

who has dispossessed himself of
everything, asking nothing for
himself—no yearning for profit
or gain. He acts as a beacon
light to others, to share his joy
for freedom from bondage,

who has conquered fear,

who is brave and invincible.
An enlightened man he is,

because he was vanquished
death and has thus reached the
consummation of his soul.

He has attained his life's destination, the highest peak of divine bliss. Having sailed across the river of life to the other shore, what else is there for him to achieve? What man could do he has done, for he is now an integral part of all creation—himself in all and all things in himself.

Other Publications by Shiv K. Kumar

Anthologies of Poems

Articulate Silences (Writers Workshop), 1970

Cobwebs in the Sun (Tata McGraw-Hill), New Delhi, 1974

Subterfuges (Oxford University Press), 1975

Woodpeckers (Sidgwick Jackson, London), 1979

Trapfalls in the Sky (Macmillan), 1986

Woolgathering (Orient Longman), 1995

Thus Spake the Buddha (UBSPD), 2001

Thus Spake Lord Krishna — a poetical transcreation of

The Bhagvad Gita (ms)

Novels

The Bone's Prayer (Arnold Heinemann), 1979

Nude Before God (Vanguard Press), New York, 1983

A River with Three Banks (UBSPD), Delhi, 1998

Infatuation (UBSPD), 2000

Two Mirrors at the Ashram (Penguin Books), 2006

Short Stories

Beyond Love & Other Stories (Vikas, New Delhi), 1980

To Nun with Love & Other Stories (Orient Longman), 2001

Play

The Last Wedding Anniversary (Macmillan), 1975

Translation

Faiz Ahmed Faiz: Selected Poems